GLOBAL ECONOMICS

Seeking a Christian Ethic

Ian McCrae

Illustrations by Dan Shepley

FRIENDSHIP PRESS • NEW YORK

Friendship Press is grateful to publishers, authors and artists for permission to reprint parts of their works. Text sources usually are cited where text appears. Other permissions are listed on page 120.

ISBN 0-377-00253-4

Copyright © 1993 by Friendship Press

Editorial Offices:
475 Riverside Drive, Room 860, New York, NY 10115-0050

Distribution Offices:
P.O. Box 37844, Cincinnati, OH 45222-0844

Manufactured in the United States of America
Printed on Recycled Paper

Library of Congress Cataloging-in-Publication Data

McCrae, I. (Ian)
    Global economics : seeking a Christian ethic : a workbook for beginners / Ian McCrae.
        p.   cm.
    Includes bibliographical references.
    ISBN 0-377-00253-4
    1. International economic relations—Religious aspects—Christianity.
2. International economic relations—Moral and ethical aspects. 3. Economics—Religious aspects--Christianity. 4. Economics—Moral and ethical aspects. I. Title.
    HF1411.M3757   1993   92-42908
    330—dc20   CIP

Contents

DEDICATION

To my wife and children
whose origins, experiences
and continuing commitments
are my best hope for
remaining sensitive to,
concerned about and involved
with our global family.

When You Read This Book, You Can Expect:

- *To feel/sense/grasp* that we really do live in an interdependent world. No individual, no group, no country can go it alone.

- *To understand* what Christian faith has to say about how we and others should use the power which money gives us.

- *To know* more about how money and power are used and misused in worldwide systems to provide life's necessities or to increase misery. Nothing about the present unjust realities in God's world is inevitable.

- *To realize* that we can make this a fairer, better world. Everyone can do something.

- *To decide* whether we want to be part of the problem or the solution. That is a decision we get to make each day.

- *To have new questions* with no easy answers. We all will continue to wrestle with these as long as we are lively Christians.

SOME BEGINNING NOTES

If you are studying this book by yourself, it is important to use it as a workbook, not a textbook. Do the exercises. Sound out some of the ideas on your family and friends even if they are not involved in the study. Try to find others who may be reading the book on their own. Most of us need some allies if we are going to try something new. Feel free to argue with the ideas presented here and work through your own understanding of the gospel's meaning in this interdependent world. Start reading the newspapers or watching television with a global awareness, especially noting economic issues. What *is* going on out there? If you are convinced that our new global awareness offers an opportunity for Christians to witness in fresh ways, take on one of the action proposals in Part 5, or come up with an idea of your own. If it doesn't work out, try something else. Every one of us can at least begin to sensitize those around us to the reality of global interdependence and to reflect on our Christian response.

Suggestions for group leaders begin on page 103.

The term "Third World" is often used to refer to countries located in Asia, Africa, Latin America, the Pacific and Middle East. This term grew out of a political debate which carved up the world into areas based on their economic status (highly industrialized and affluent vs. less affluent and less industrialized). The "First World" consisted of most of what at the time was Western Europe, the U.S., Canada, Japan, etc. "Third World/First World" distinctions are highly problematic. For one, the diversity of economies and their relative affluence even within geographical regions makes it difficult to so easily divide the world into so few categories. Moreover, many find the distinction conveys an undesirable impression of a social/cultural hierarchy and that the implicit goal is for the "Third World" to become like those in the "First World." Furthermore, it disguises the fact that in terms of world population, the "Third World" would come closer to being the "Two-Thirds World." Thus, more people are beginning to use the term "South" (south of the equator) and "North" even though these are flawed terms as well. Language—the power to name and define--is just as critical an issue in talking about economics as it is in other areas of life.

1

What's Going On in the World?

Stories and exercises about our interdependent world

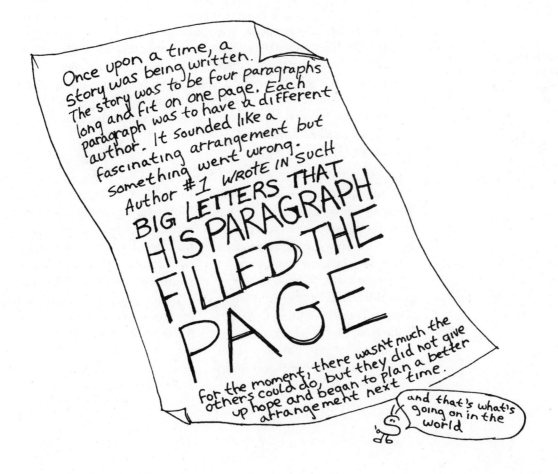

Once upon a time, a story was being written. The story was to be four paragraphs long and fit on one page. Each paragraph was to have a different author. It sounded like a fascinating arrangement but something went wrong.

Author #1 WROTE IN SUCH BIG LETTERS THAT HIS PARAGRAPH FILLED THE PAGE

For the moment, there wasn't much the others could do, but they did not give up hope and began to plan a better arrangement next time.

and that's what's going on in the world

On a typical day, as you read your newspaper, scan a magazine or listen to the radio, you will unwittingly be putting together a business report that reads something like this:

1. Beginning in 1990, Northern Telecom, a Canadian corporation, sold to its customers in the United States telecommunication equipment made by a Japanese firm at its plant in North Carolina. 2. The chief exporter of computers from Japan is IBM. 3. The largest employer in Singapore is General Electric. 4. Pepsi Cola will invest $8 million to build plants, fast food restaurants and distribution systems in Spain. 5. Airbus Industrie, a four-country European producer of commercial aircraft whose planes take off or land somewhere in the world every 30 seconds, advertised that it has contributed more than $3.5 billion to the American economy, creating thousands of jobs in more than 30 states.

***

November 20, 1991—McDonnell Douglas announced today that it is selling 40% of its commercial aircraft business for $2 billion. The buyer is Taiwan Aerospace but companies in Japan and South Korea will also be involved. News of the sale caused a sharp jump in the value of McDonnell Douglas stock. McDonnell is the largest defense contractor in the USA. The Pentagon which formerly has objected to such arrangements by any of its suppliers made no statement although some members of Congress raised objections. The spokesperson for the company said, "This is our effort to make ourselves a stronger and more competitive company." In answer to the criticism that the sale would mean a loss of American jobs, the spokesperson said that without such foreign investment, a new generation of aircraft would remain on paper and no domestic jobs would be created. However observers noted that many of the sub-suppliers would no longer be U.S. firms. (*Christian Science Monitor*, 27 November 1991)

***

Global Economic Snapshots: 1. Hospital patient records from Pomona, California, or Greensboro, North Carolina, are transferred from information on paper to computer files at an office in Manila, the Philippines. 2. Manhole covers for Phoenix, Arizona, or Newport News, Virginia are made in India. 3. Shoe repair shops in Florida have their work done in the Yucatan Peninsula of Mexico. (*Entangling Alliances*, John Maxwell Hamilton, Seven Locks Press, Washington, D.C., 1990)

A young East German who visited Hungary before East German borders opened to the West delighted in some consumer products which have become symbols of Western society, "Coca Cola is great. McDonald's is great. Playboy is great. There is nothing like this in the East. The West is great!" (*Conflicts of Interest: Canada and the Third World*, Jamie Swift and Brian Tomlinson, eds., p. 19)

Robert H. Galvin, chairman of Motorola, has announced that if it is necessary to close some of their factories, it would not automatically close its Southeast Asian plants before its American ones. "We need our Far Eastern customers and we cannot alienate the Malaysians. We must treat our employees all over the world equally." (*The Work of Nations*, Robert Reich, p. 143)

WHAT'S GOING ON IN THE WORLD?

The economic walls of nationhood are tumblin' down!

What in the world *is* going on?

TRY THIS EXERCISE

Jot down two or three ideas about the causes and some possible solutions for the following problems:

THE DRUG PROBLEM

Causes   Possible Solutions

UNEMPLOYMENT IN CANADA/USA

Causes   Possible Solutions

FAMILY FARM FORECLOSURES

Causes   Possible Solutions

THE 1990 - ? RECESSION

Causes   Possible Solutions

Bangalore, India: This pleasant city in southern India is becoming a global center for the computer industry. The managing director for Texas Instruments explained: "India is part of a strategic presence. In the long-term, we are interested in the larger markets of South and Southeast Asia as well as the Pacific." The city has attracted many of India's best scientific minds. Their talents and relatively low salaries—less than the minimum wage in the USA—have caused an increasing number of Indian and multinational computer companies to establish plants here. The influx of business has transformed a "sleepy haven for pensioners into a traffic-clogged city of four million." (*New York Times*, 6 October, 1991, F9)

★

TRY THIS EXERCISE

As you thought about these problems, you might have found a common element in both the causes and possible solutions. A global dimension is involved.

Obviously, the supply side of the drug question involves the nations of Southeast Asia and Latin America. Unemployment in Canada or the United States is related to such issues as free trade between our countries, movement of factories to low-wage regions of the world, international competition in the marketplace.

As Latin America slumped under its debt crisis in the 1980s, many nations could no longer afford to buy farm equipment from the U.S., contributing to the rural slump there. Then, as Latin American nations expanded agricultural exports to pay off their foreign debt, Canadian and US producers found more competition for their world markets.

A recession is clearly related to many of these same issues. In the United States, the budget deficit, created chiefly through vast increases in military expenditures to protect against "the enemy," has sharply limited those government expenditures that might spur economic growth and create jobs.

And just as the causes of these problems have global dimensions, so any realistic solutions will have to consider global approaches.

Make a list of 15 materials that are part of your home and its furnishings, including any material used in your clothing. Then list 10 foods you have on hand. As you think about the source of these goods and materials, how many countries are represented? Make a list.

Materials	Source/Country

Food	Source/Country

You can do it! It's not that tough!

★

Does your list look anything like this?

Materials	Source/Country
Copper wiring	Zambia
Aluminum	Argentina
Rubber	Thailand
Dog food	Peru
TV	Taiwan
Sugar	Dominican Republic
Tomatoes in March	Mexico
Coffee	Colombia, El Salvador
Silk	China
Baseball	Costa Rica, Haiti

WHAT'S GOING ON IN THE WORLD?

We are riding in the same boat, and we will sink or sail together.

NOTE TO GROUP LEADERS

If you are leading a study with more than 20 participants, and have a significant amount of time for research, discussion and analysis, you may want to engage your group in the exercise outlined on pp. 106-108

Times of Crisis

What in the world *is* going on?

In recent years, thousands of Bolivians have moved to the eastern slopes of the Andes to grow or process coca leaves for the drug cartels. Many of them worked in the tin mines, but in the mid-1980s, 20,000 miners lost their jobs when the world tin market collapsed as other products were substituted in manufacturing. Since colonial days, Bolivia's economy has been geared to providing raw materials for the industrialized countries. Some of the miners who tried farming discovered that they could not cover their costs of production with "legal" crops. Jose Vargas, who works in the jungle at night stomping barefoot in a plastic vat of kerosene and coca leaves until dawn, knows he is endangering his life. "If there was work, we wouldn't come here to crush coca leaves. But I'd rather die of a police bullet than starve."

(*Latinamerica Press*, 29 September 1988, quoted in "Intricate Web: Drugs and the Economic Crisis" by Bishop Felton Edwin May, 1990)

* * *

Pierre is 12 years old. One day a man came to his Haitian village and told him that he could earn American dollars for collecting eggs in a henhouse. That sounded good so Pierre climbed into the truck where he was soon joined by other children, some as young as 8 years, and by young men who were also following the promise of paid work. They travelled east and soon crossed the border into the Dominican Republic. There they were turned over to men in uniforms who gave each of them a piece of paper called a "contract." Pierre, who could not read, was told to put his thumbprint on the paper.

Pierre and some of the others were then taken to what he recognized as a sugar plantation. He was given a machete which was half as tall as he was and told to begin cutting the cane. He worked twelve hours a day, seven days a week on this government-owned plantation. He lived with other children in a concrete, overcrowded barracks without drinking water, electricity, cooking facilities or toilets. There was no education provided and health care was offered only for extreme emergencies. Pierre never saw any money and at the end of the six months' harvest season, he had nothing. He was then trucked back to Haiti.

The Dominican government claims that since 1990 all workers' rights are respected but observers on the field say little has changed. The U.S. Trade Representative accepted the word of the Dominican government and continued to grant it trade benefits. As of 1992, the United States has made no attempt to pressure the Dominican Republic to improve its practices.

(Information from the Lawyers Committee for Human Rights, New York).

A Conversation from the Philippines

I HAVE TO CLIMB FOUR FLIGHTS OF STAIRS TO MY HOTEL ROOM.

My children have to walk five kilometers to school. They can't attend much during rainy season.

MY SHOWER DOESN'T WORK.

We have one water pump for 83 families.

IT'S NOISY. I CAN HEAR THE RADIO IN THE ROOM NEXT DOOR.

The military came shooting and terrorizing. They took my husband while we pleaded that he was not a guerrilla.

MY FAN DIDN'T WORK DURING THE FOUR-HOUR BROWN-OUT.

We hope some day to have electricity.

THEY DON'T EVEN COME IN EACH DAY AND CLEAN MY ROOM.

My wife and sometimes the children have to help harvest in order for us to survive. The cane cuts into their hands.

I HOPE THAT $50 WILL GET US A ROOM WITH PRIVATE BATH AND AIR CONDITIONER.

My feet are swollen. The children's stomachs sometimes swell when they do not get enough to eat.

(Mae Lord in *The Christian Century*, 7 November 1990, p. 1033, adapted)

* * *

"Good news! The winter rains are ending Chile's three-year drought! We hope the rain means more sanitary food and drinking water, for sanitation is key to the fight against the cholera epidemic here. The heavy rains were bad news for some of Chile's northern desert, however. Many places received 100 times the normal yearly rainfall in only 24 hours. The floods and mud slides in Antofagasta claimed 150 lives, left 20,000 homeless and damaged 6,000 homes in two days.

The Good News of God and the Shalom of God's creation mean salvation from poverty, misery and death. This message leads the victims of these disasters, and those who accompany them, to denounce the irresponsibility of those in power as the tragedies' main cause.

Natural or divine forces did not cause Antofagasta's heavy losses. This Pacific port city, built at the foot of badly eroded hills, received only 14 millimeters of rain (about one-half inch). The problem was that Antofagasta's poorly constructed water system broke apart.

The water company, privatized under Pinochet's dictatorship, built second-rate installations for profit's sake. International monetary institutions pressure Latin American governments to reduce quality control regulations in construction and other industries for foreign investment's sake. But who defends the interests of the people of Antofagasta?

And who defends the Andean peoples from the cholera that reappeared in 1991 after a 100-year absence? Peru reports 200,000 cases and 1,300 deaths; Ecuador, 8,000 cases; Colombia, 1,500. Chile and Brazil report outbreaks; Argentina, Uruguay and Paraguay fear it will break out soon.

Cholera is a disease of the poor. A healthy person's stomach acids can kill the 'vibrio cholerae' bacteria but a malnourished or sick person's acids cannot. Persons contract it by ingesting tiny pieces of feces infected with cholera.

Throughout Andean America, untreated sewer water flows through canals and rivers into the Pacific. Too often, farmers have no choice but to use this water to irrigate their crops. Another main source of contamination is through the scarcity of treated drinking water. Forty per cent of Lima's seven million people do not have access to clean water. The Panamerican Health Organization estimates that Peru must invest $320 million per year for 10 years in order to provide water and sanitary services for its inhabitants. Peru has only $31 million available, which will not even keep up with Peru's demographic growth; and at the same time international banks are threatening to cut off Peru from future loans unless it cuts back public services even further. Such human-produced conditions foster cholera's spread."

(June 1991 newsletter from Jane and George Sullivan-Davis, seconded by the Disciples of Christ to the National Council of Churches)

* * *

"Our children are dying so our countries can pay their international debts." —a Venezuelan economist
(*World Encounter*, ELCA, No. 4, 1989, p. 22)

* * *

"Our days of living from pay check to pay check are over ... I was laid-off."

"We're always asking ourselves, we housewives: What did we do that we have to pay this foreign debt? Is it that our children have eaten too much? . . . Or gone to the best schools? . . . Worn the best clothes . . . Or have our salaries been too high? . . . Have we better houses? . . . We all shout in unison: No! So who has benefited? Why are we the ones to have to pay that debt?"—a Bolivian housewife

(*The International Debt Crisis*, Canadian Taskforce of the Churches and Corporate Responsibility, July 1989)

* * *

WHAT'S GOING ON IN THE WORLD?

Of the world's 5.2 billion people, 1.5 billion do not have even the basic necessities of life. They live in absolute poverty.

According to the United Nations Food and Agriculture Organization, there are 786 million chronically undernourished people in the developing countries (although this is a drop from 20 years ago, when there were 941 million).

200 million people are at risk of going blind from Vitamin A deficiency.

300 million people have annual incomes of $100 or less (30 cents a day).

40,000 are children who were alive 24 hours ago. One child under the age of five dies every two seconds. And they die one at a time. Parents in Canada or the United States face odds of 1 in 100 of one of their children dying in the first year. In a dozen African countries, the odds are about 30 in 100.

100 million children under the age of 16 live on the streets of the world's cities. In Sao Paulo, Brazil, human rights groups estimate that on every day in recent years, the police beat to death one young person to make him confess to crimes he probably did not commit.

In a number of countries in Africa and Latin America, average incomes have fallen 25 percent since 1980.

In the poorest countries of the world, spending on health has dropped 50 percent and on education by 25 percent since 1980.

In nearly half of the world's developing countries, primary school enrollment is dropping.

* * *

One of the tragedies of today's world is that by the time you read this book, all of these numbers will have increased.

"Life is unbearable."—a Zambian farmer

(*Christian Science Monitor*, 18 November 1991)

(Unfortunately, the newly elected government has been ordered by the International Monetary Fund and the World Bank to remove corn subsidies and cut back on human service programs. For a while at least, life will be even more unbearable.)

* * *

"It is difficult even to think of [the collapse of the Bank of Credit and Commerce International]; it means that our project will have to close. This is the present and the future of homeless children in Sudan. Hundreds of kids who were served by our project will now have to go back [to the streets]. You cannot stand seeing all your children dying in front of you." —the director of the Sabah project in Khartoum, Sudan

(*Christian Science Monitor*, 23 July 1991)

* * *

"The overall situation couldn't be worse for these countries [Ethiopia, Sudan, Somalia, Mozambique, Liberia, Angola]. Every minute, every hour there is a delay, hope dims and lives are being lost."—Director-General, U.N. Food and Agricultural Organization

(*Christian Science Monitor*, 25 June 1991)

* * *

"In 1991, a cyclone ripped through Bangladesh, killing more than 139,000 people. But each year, even without a cyclone, diarrhea kills 260,000 children under the age of 5; respiratory infections kill another 157,000 each year, and measles kills 60,000 children."

(*The New York Times*, 19 May 1991)

* * *

"From a very young age I have known poverty. I grew up in a squatter community, and I am sick and tired of enduring hardships. I want a better life for my children and will die, if necessary, to achieve that."—a Filipina mother

(*This Land Was Ours*, Charles W. Bailey, New York: Harper Collins, 1991)

Signs of Hope

What in the world *is* going on?

In 1974, the Marcos government in the Philippines began a project funded by the World Bank to build hydro-electric dams on 3,400 square kilometers of land on which tribal peoples lived. It was to be one of the world's largest dam projects and was to provide power for multinational corporations and nearby cities. Ms. Francisca Macli-ing, a member of the Bontoc Igorot people, testified at a World Council of Churches hearing about what such a proposal meant to the indigenous people.

"Land is life. These are our ancestral lands. When the government wanted to build the four dams along the Chico River, it meant the death of our people. We really had to fight it because it meant displacement of almost all the villages of the Kalingas and the Bontocs and, of course, aside from the ancestral lands, the loss of our rice fields, our rice terraces, and our kaingins (small plots of land)."

And fight it they did! Coming together in an unprecedented display of unity, the tribes drafted a statement of formal agreement of their position and began a sustained opposition. They won support of church leaders in the Philippines and sympathetic groups around the world. A battalion of the Philippine army was sent into the area, which led to numerous human rights violations. Despite these, the campaign continued. In a few years, it was obvious that the project could not go ahead and all of the equipment and construction workers were removed from the area. Small wonder that Francisca told that story with pride.

(Source: World Council of Churches, Churches Commission on Peace and Development, Debt Resource Materials No. 2, "Ecumenical Hearing on the International Monetary System and the Churches' Responsibility, 21-24 August 1988, West Berlin")

* * *

"In many parts of Ethiopia there are springs and small streams that can be developed for irrigation in dry farming areas," says John Schutte, financial coordinator in Ethiopia for the Lutheran World Federation (LWF).

Four years ago, when employees of the LWF proposed the idea of diverting a stream to provide irrigation to this once-empty site, local farmers were skeptical.

"'How can water pass through the rocky areas of the mountain?' they asked," says Tesfaye Demissie, of the LWF office in the city of Dire Diawa, about 20 miles from here. "They didn't believe it. But later on, after a year, after our work was completed, they appreciated and admired [the project]," he says.

Instead of coming in and building a canal, LWF offered food to farmers in the area in exchange for the work needed to build the canal. Such a scheme is popularly known as "food for work," a concept widely used in developing countries, with wheat and other grain, usually from North America or Europe.

The one-year construction began in 1986. As the canal passes bridge-like over deep gullies, it reminds visitors of a miniature Roman aqueduct. It runs nearly two miles from the stream.

"Somehow, without blasting anything, just using hand tools, we have done this canal," Mr. Demissie says proudly. "It works very well, since for the last four years, we've never seen any damage or a crack. So that shows the work is strong enough."

At first, some 250 acres were irrigated. But it became apparent that, if more water were available, up to 650 acres could be irrigated. Local residents told the LWF staff about a spring some six miles up in the hills. Like many springs in Ethiopia, it was not developed. . . . With more "food for work," residents constructed a channel for the stream water to reach the village.

Many of the families who worked on the project have moved here. The population of Gerame today is around 600, about the maximum number of people who can live here, given the still-limited water supply.

Khadija Adam Wariyo's mud home is just a few feet from the canal. She and her family used to live over one of the hills behind the village.

"There was no rain over there," she says, pointing toward her old home. "This is better. My family is harvesting here, and I have food for work.

"I get three crops a year," she continues, after adjusting to the surprise of a foreign visitor. "Sorghum, corn, bananas, and sweet potatoes. Where I was living before, we got only one crop a year."

Another refreshing sight here is the fruit trees around many of the homes: Bananas and papayas are favorites. They're kept alive in the harsh climate by water hauled from the canal by hand in plastic jugs. Mohammed Beriko says his standard of living has improved since he moved here. "When we first came down here, we were starved. We got food for work, and helped ourselves. We built better homes here and we have enough food to eat now."

LWF has sponsored 25 other village projects like this one in the region. Mr. Schutte says others are under way elsewhere in Ethiopia. Each one costs a maximum of $75,000, he says. The costs for this village figure out to about $100 per village resident over the four-year period.

Some "food for work" is still paid to a few residents to water trees planted on a nearby hillside for future firewood use, and for operating a small tree nursery to supply other projects.

Schutte says only a shortage of international donations is keeping LWF from carrying out even more village oasis projects in Ethiopia. (*Christian Science Monitor*, 5 June 1991, p. 12)

* * *

The Third-World debt crisis has been particularly hard on women, whose home labors have not diminished but who have had to work increased hours at lower wages to help their families survive. But women are responding to these problems in creative ways. In Lima, Peru, there are more and more community kitchens. Women bring their meager food supplies together and take turns preparing the meals for all of the families. They stretch the food budget, gain time for additional money-making activities, and build communities of support. (WCC, CCPD Debt Resource Materials #1)

* * *

In North Carolina, three universities have created a Center for World Environment and Sustainable Development. Pedro Sanchez, director of the Center, recognizes the values both of tropical forests and of the local farmers' need to grow crops. He feels that the Center will have shown the value of its work when the farmers have sustainable agriculture under way and there is also national park development. Says Sanchez: "Our goal is to work ourselves out of these jobs, to empower the local people." (*Christian Science Monitor*, 22 July 1991)

When third world production of coffee skyrocketed and prices plunged, some farmers in Costa Rica looked for an alternative. They found it in growing decorative plants which on the same amount of land, produced returns 25 times greater than for coffee. Encouraged by government policies and technical know-how from the U.S. Agency for International Development, the farmers export both to North America and to Europe. "We're always looking for new customers." (*Christian Science Monitor*, 4 September 1991)

Here is a short sampler of diverse ways in which people are working together for social-economic justice and sustainable development.

THE GLOBAL FORUM

For two weeks in June 1992, 29,000 participants from 171 countries, representing roughly 9,000 organizations, attended the "Global Forum" in Rio de Janeiro, Brazil. This non-official conference was held in tandem with the official United Nation's Conference on Environment and Sustainable Development (popularly known as the "Earth Summit").

Citizens from around the world came together to discuss how they could help make environmentally sound development and economic justice a reality. They discussed and debated what kinds of changes would be required in their personal lives, in public policy, in the behavior of businesses—particularly multinational corporations, and in the role of international institutions such as the World Bank and United Nations.

To sharpen and concretize these discussions, many participated in the drafting of 30 non-governmental organization treaties. Some topics were parallel to what the official governments were discussing (e.g. biodiversity) while most covered topics that the official proceedings avoided—militarism, trade, women, population, consumption patterns, sustainable agriculture, etc. Each set of negotiations had co-facilitators representing a South and North perspective and teams consisted of volunteers from both the North and South committed to giving much time and energy to the project. Discussions were held in many languages, with translation available in the more common languages.

Individual participants could then sign the treaties on behalf of themselves or their organizations, committing themselves to agreeing at least with the principles embodied and to further collaborative work with others who signed the treaty. The treaties are available as educational and organizing tools for anyone who would like to use them.

(The treaties have been gathered into a looseleaf notebook, available for $20 from Sharyle Patton, Commonweal, Box 316, Bolinas, CA 94924. Telephone (415) 868-0970. Fax (415) 868-2230. For more information in Canada, contact:

Sophia Murphy, CCIC, 1 Nicholas Street, Suite 300, Ottawa, Ontario, Canada. Telephone: (613) 236-4547. Fax: (613) 236-2188.)

DEVELOPMENT ALTERNATIVES WITH WOMEN FOR A NEW ERA

Women activists, researchers, advocates, public policy makers in the South organized around the Nairobi UN conference in 1985 to strengthen their own voices for change. As a result they have built regional coalitions and an inter-regional network across Asia, the Pacific, Africa, the Middle East, Latin America and the Caribbean. DAWN members do research, and organizing and try to influence public policy in home countries and in the major power centers. They are committed to developing models of development which are sustainable, promote cultural integrity and are equitable and liberating for women, men and children.

DAWN hosted an international workshop for women from the South in 1992 to see what the participants might do to try to overcome the technical and financial limitations that women of the South face in terms of access to information and communications. After four days of work, the participants launched a fax information exchange, WOMENET. This is designed to help disseminate the views of and information from women of the South to each other, women's organizations across the globe, mainstream media, etc.

(For more information, contact Anne Walker, The International Women's Tribune Centre, 777 UN Plaza, New York, NY 10017, USA. Telephone: (212) 687-8633. Fax: (212) 661-2704.)

COALITION FOR JUSTICE IN THE MAQUILADORAS

One Catholic sister, Susan Mika, with a passion for justice and a dream, succeeded in building what is now a strong and large network to improve conditions along both sides of the U.S.-Mexico border. The Coalition for Justice in the Maquiladoras ("CJM") is a bi-national group of sixty religious, environmental, community, labor, women's and Latino organizations.

The group sponsors an ongoing campaign to press U.S. multinational corporations to adopt socially responsible business practices in the maquiladora (special assembly factories in Mexico) sector. CJM developed a Code of Standards of Conduct which covers corporate environmental contamination, health and safety practices, fair employment practices and standards of living, and community impact. Through such tactics as shareholder resolutions, they have already won some wage increases, release of environmental information to enable workers and community residents to more effectively protect themselves against hazards, and some environmental clean-up.

While the focus is on U.S. corporations because they are the lion's share of companies operating in this zone, the concerns are equally applicable to Canadian companies, more of which are moving operations to Mexico.

(For more information, contact: CJM, c/o Benedictine Resource Center, 530 Bandera Road, San Antonio, Texas 78228. Telephone: (512) 735-4988.)

THE FREEDOM FROM DEBT COALITION

One of the oldest, best organized and most successful groups working on the issue of foreign debt in their own country is this Filipino coalition. A rainbow of groups—peasants, workers, students, women, academics, peace activists, religious groups, teachers—pursue a broad range of activities.

They work to educate Filipinos about the extent of their country's debt crisis and its implications for their daily lives. Some members try to track where the loan money actually went in order to see what was "legitimate" and "illegitimate." They want to raise the question about the morality of having to pay back loans which went for socially irresponsible purposes (e.g. a nuclear power plant with a troubled construction history which was built near an earthquake fault line) or to line a wealthy individual's pocket.

Another process initiated has been a national series of small meetings whereby Filipinos formulate their own ideas for what their community needs to develop and be sustainable. The results have been accumulated into an alternative plan for bioregional development. Some members of the Coalition are working with partners in Europe and North America to convince international development banks, governments and aid agencies to try and fund this development model rather than that currently promoted and financed.

(For more information, contact Chris Coburn, Columban Campaign on Debt and Development Alternatives, c/o Friends of the Earth, 218 D Street Southeast, Washington, D.C. 20003. Telephone: (202) 544-2600 ext. 208.)

WHAT'S GOING ON IN THE WORLD?

People are confronting their own problems with creativity and courage. Sometimes they are being helped by persons and institutions who understand that:

- People must be involved in designing and implementing their own solutions.
- Technology must be adapted to fit the situation.
- Greater self-sufficiency is an essential goal. That may mean growing their own food crops or increasing family income through new work opportunities.
- Women play a central role in successful development projects.
- Even the grimmest situations contain the seeds of hope.

Points of Beginning

The present global economic and financial arrangements are a disaster for much of the world's peoples and a theological and ethical crisis for Christians. While one should not jump too easily from biblical parables to present day realities, the judgment scene described by Jesus (Matthew 25:31-46) is strongly suggestive. The hungry are not fed; the naked are not clothed; the homeless are not housed. The nations of the world have been brought before the court of justice and have been found wanting. And no appeal to the purity of their motives or their public statements can change that verdict.

But hope continues to break through. Proponents of massive technological projects are no longer able to build first and ask questions later. A huge hydro-electric power project planned by HydroQuebec on the Great Whale River has run into stiff opposition from the Cree and Inuit people who live in the area and from environmental groups and church groups in Canada and the United States. The proposed purchase of energy by New York State has been cancelled. The project may be completed but corporations are having to face their responsibilities both to people and to nature in a new way.

Educators are speaking out on the importance of global thinking. The president of Harvard University, Neil Rudenstine, believes that "there's a capacity now to think about, learn about, and be impressed by what is happening all over the world, at any given moment—to be able to get to any part of the world at any given moment almost instantaneously. Students have to think about what forces are in motion at what speed and velocity, and how to deal with them. . . . In this interlocked world, if you want to do something to an economy, it's no longer a bilateral or even a trilateral situation . . . We have to help students to be much more adaptable intellectually—that is, we have to help them to think about the whole world in a way that's going to demand over time, the capacity to deal with quite accelerated change in a complexity of systems." (*Christian Science Monitor*, 18 October 1991, p. 12)

Military aircraft whose reconnaisance missions once were limited to spying on the enemy are now used in a program called "confidence-building measures" (CBMs). For example, they monitor troop movements between Israel and Syria, providing the same information to both sides. CBMs also include regular meetings of top military and foreign policy personnel between nations to exchange information and address potential tension spots. Some feel that the 1990s will be the "decade of confidence-building measures." (*Christian Science Monitor*, 24 September 1992)

And Christians around the world are asking tough questions, analyzing both the biblical and the economic issues involved, suggesting creative new approaches with what might be called prophetic realism.

But what about us, laity and clergy, in the congregations in Canada and the United States? If we have not thought much about the global economy, or its impact, our reactions may be:

1. This has nothing to do with me.

2. It's all too complicated to understand.

3. Even if I could figure it out, there's nothing I can do about it.

4. I don't believe the Christian faith has a major concern for such matters.

Or, our reactions may be:

1. Global interdependence may be the most personally relevant fact of our time.

2. The main ideas about the global economy are understandable to almost anyone.

3. Every concerned person can do something.

4. The issues involved in the global economy go to the very heart of our faith.

Henri J.M. Nouwen, scholar and friend of the poor, said:

"You are Christian only so long as you constantly pose critical questions to the society you live in, so long as you emphasize the need of conversion both for yourself and for the world, so long as you in no way let yourself become established in the situation of the world, so long as you stay unsatisfied with the status quo and keep saying that a new world is yet to come. You are Christian only when you believe you have a role to play in the realization of the new kingdom, and when you urge everyone you meet with holy unrest to make haste so that the promise might be soon fulfilled, so long as you live as a Christian you keep looking for a new order, a new structure, a new life." (*Creative Ministry*, Henri J.M. Nouwen [New York: Doubleday, 1978], 88-89.)

If you become involved in thinking about or acting on global economic issues, you may be in the minority in your congregation and in your community. As the American novelist Flannery O'Connor once said, "You will know the truth, and the truth will make you odd." But oddness can add meaning and excitement to your life. After all, don't we worship the One who "makes all things new?"

"I don't see why all this should be our problem."

2

What Does Christian Faith Have to Say?

Bible study and ways to apply Scripture to daily actions

"And may we continue to be worthy of consuming a disproportionate share of this planet's resources."

Drawing by Lorenz, © 1992 The New Yorker Magazine, Inc.

How Does Christian Faith Speak?

So how do we feel about what's going on in our world, that is, in God's world? What are we to think about it? Can we do anything to change that world? Does our Christian faith help us to evaluate our feelings, our thoughts, our actions? Does our faith help us to see new possibilities?

Suppose a clerk at the supermarket checkout counter gives you change for $20 instead of the $10 you actually gave her. Surely Christian faith gives a clear answer as to what to do. In this case, Christian faith is like a blueprint providing a specific and detailed picture of how to build our lives.

But let's imagine an individual or family building a budget. Is not Christian faith, in this case, more like a road sign pointing to our destination or like a compass that lets us check if we are heading in the right direction?

At times, technical questions arise. What happens to the economy if interest rates are lowered by half a percent? Debate on that subject could be lively and important since the move would affect the lives of millions of people. But, on a specific problem like this, other than insisting that the participants should be honest and thorough in their research and discussion, Christian faith offers no further advice.

Christian faith sometimes offers specific guidance; at other times, faith points us in a direction and we must find the best route; in some situations, Christian faith remains silent.

When Christians are asked how they know what is right or wrong, they tend to answer that they rely on the Bible, tradition, reason, and experience:

1. What does the Bible teach us?

2. What has the church through the centuries understood to be the Christian way of living?

3. What insights come from careful thinking, as an individual or together in Christian fellowship?

4. Does our experience and the experience of other Christians affirm the rightness of our decision?

These four questions have been compared to the legs of a chair. Some Christians feel strongly that the Bible is most important. Other equally sincere and informed Christians argue that all four legs need to be firmly in place to avoid a tippy uncertainty. But all Christians are united in their conviction that without the Bible, there is no Christian faith at all. And what follows is that

WITHOUT A KNOWLEDGE OF THE BIBLE, CHURCH MEMBERS CANNOT FEEL, THINK, OR ACT AS CHRISTIANS!

Unfortunately, many Christians are somewhat casual in their approach to Bible study. Such an approach will not do if we want the Bible to help us reach decisions about right and wrong.

Of course, people who profess to know the Bible do not always read its message the same way. Frank Chikane, general secretary of the South African Council of Churches, tells of being arrested for his leadership in the struggle for equal rights in South Africa. While in detention, he was tortured twice. The torture was supervised by a member of his own denomination. Says Chikane, "When both the tortured and the torturer are appealing to the same book as the basis for their action, then you need to say more than 'I believe in the Bible.'"

Inspired by Scripture, "true believers" have had some high moments and produced exemplary witnesses to the Christian gospel. But Bible-believing Christians have also stood by and even participated while whole peoples were enslaved and cultures destroyed. The Bible's ability to motivate persons to act is not in question; that those actions will always reflect the spirit and teachings of Jesus Christ is less certain.

Nevertheless, we'd better study it!

We read it not to win a Bible quiz contest nor even because it is our Christian duty. We read it to find "the subtle intersection between the text and our own life where the sparks fly, the insights are born, the corner is turned—where, in short, we find the living God addressing us at the point of our and the world's need." (*Transforming Bible Study,* Walter Wink [Nashville,Tenn: Abingdon Press, 1980])

KUDZU

How do we study the Bible?

Principle #1:
Context

The biblical context of the passage is important for understanding its meaning.

What was the main question/situation which called forth this teaching or story? What did this passage mean to its first hearers?

You may find it helpful to use a Bible commentary to learn more about the various theories on who wrote the passage, to whom, when, where, and why. Although uncertainties remain, scholars have reached widespread agreement on many of these questions.

For example, you would need to apply this principle as you study the parable of the workers in the vineyard (Matthew 20:1-11). Without an understanding of its context, this parable can be misinterpreted as suggesting a rather strange economic arrangement. Once the context is understood— Do Jews and gentiles come into the realm of God on the same terms?— the point of the story becomes clear.

Principle #2:
Unequal Relevance

The Bible is not a "level" book. All of its teachings are not of equal religious insight nor of equal relevance for our lives. When the Bible differs with itself, how do we deal with the difference? How do we decide which verses take precedence over others?

Some Christians feel that if we had sufficient understanding, all apparent contradictions would disappear. But for this workbook, we will assume that not all biblical teachings are of equal relevance for living today. There are differences. For example, the Bible is not consistent in its teaching about how our enemies should be treated (see Psalm 137:8-9, Proverbs 25:21 and Matthew 5:43-44).

When the ethical content of different biblical passages seems to diverge, Christians will ask the extent to which these passages reflect the mind and spirit of Jesus Christ as that is revealed in Scripture. In that sense, the Bible provides the criterion to evaluate itself.

Principle #3:
Truth embodied

Scripture helps us to discover the nature of God, God's relationship with us, and our relationship with one another and with the wider universe.

We need to figure out how to live in our time. We have to distinguish between the eternal truths in the Bible and the particular application of those truths in a given time, place or situation. For example, while the Bible clearly affirms the worth and dignity of all persons, it seems to accept the practice of slavery (seeking to transform rather than abolish that practice).

We will not agree on every application of theological affirmations we find in Scripture. But we are free to struggle together to understand how eternal biblical truths can become real in our time.

BIZARRO By DAN PIRARO

Principle #4:
Vision

The Bible seldom provides specific rules which apply in every situation but does give us a vision of God's will for us.

For example, consider the teachings given by Jesus in the Sermon on the Mount (Matt. 5:38-42).

Cheeks should not always be turned; evildoers must be resisted; cloaks should not always be given away; not every request from a borrower should be honored. Neither our experience nor our common sense will support a literal interpretation of this passage as a guide for our actions. But if this is not a specific rule to live by, then what value do such passages have for us?

Passages like the one from the Sermon on the Mount suggest that part of a new vision which comes through Jesus Christ is that we are not to be bound by narrow rules of conduct as to what is right and wrong. The importance of having a vision of how life ought to be lived can hardly be overestimated. It is a vision which will always summon us beyond what we are doing and even beyond what we want to do.

What does the Bible say?

Even if Christians are not in complete agreement as to how the Bible is to be studied and do not talk about its authority in the same way, nevertheless there is much that we can affirm together.

We accept that:

■ Jesus Christ is the Son of God, our Lord and Savior.

■ We are to love God and to love our neighbors as we love ourselves.

■ We have been given a ministry of reconciliation.

TRY THIS EXERCISE

On the next few pages, you will find six groups of Scripture passages. As you read each group, look for a common theme that suggests a direction or guide for living today. After you've thought about the passages, jot down your ideas in the space provided. Then read the comments that follow.

At the end, we will list six biblical "pointers," but you may add others. As we explore the various questions of global economics, these pointers will be our measuring rods, the criteria by which we will make our decisions and take our actions as Christians.

TRY THIS EXERCISE: *Group 1*

I will make with them a covenant of peace and banish wild animals from the land, so that they may live in the wild and sleep in the woods securely. I will make them and the region around my hill a blessing; and I will send down the showers in their season; they shall be showers of blessing. The trees of the field shall yield their fruit, and the earth shall yield its increase. They shall be secure on their soil. (Ezek. 35:25-27a)

* * *

See, the home of God is among mortals. He will dwell with them as their God; they will be his peoples, and God himself will be with them; he will wipe every tear from their eyes. Death will be no more; mourning and crying and pain will be no more . . . (Rev. 21:2-4)

* * *

By the waters of Babylon—there we sat down and there we wept when we remembered Zion. On the willows there we hung up our harps. For there our captors asked us for songs, and our tormentors asked for mirth, saying, "Sing us one of the songs of Zion!" How could we sing the Lord's song in a foreign land? (Ps. 137:1-4)

* * *

These are the words of the letter that the prophet Jeremiah sent from Jerusalem to the remaining elders among the exiles, and to the priests, the prophets and all the people . . . Seek the welfare of the city where I have sent you into exile, and pray to the Lord on its behalf, for in its welfare, you will find your welfare. (Jer. 29:1, 7)

* * *

One common theme in these passages is that God has a vision for how the world should be. To have a vision can make all the difference in life, as the following story shows!

Dom Helder Camara was the Archbishop in Recife, a very poor community on Brazil's northeastern coast. He usually rode public transportation as he carried out his duties. One morning he found himself seated opposite an eight-year-old boy and asked him where he was going. "I'm taking my ant for a ride," said the boy, holding up a stick on which, indeed, an ant was riding. Dom Helder writes that he decided to tell the boy about his own ants at home. He told how occasionally he had to get an agreement with them that he would put out a pot of honey if they would leave his roses alone. The little boy did not think this was unusual. It was the most natural conversation in the world. Of course one could talk to ants! So Dom Helder told about finding Ant Claudia one day limping though the garden.

Wanting to help, he picked her up to look at her sore feet, turned her over—and she saw the sky for the first time! Writes Dom Helder: "I soon realized that there was no point in asking her about her foot. She wasn't listening. She was looking at the sky." She had a new vision of the possibilities in life!

(from *A Thousand Reasons for Living*, Dom Helder Camara, ed. Jose de Broucker, trans. Alan Neame, Fortress Press, 1981, pp. 5-7)

What common theme do you find in these scriptures?

★

The biblical words for the vision are **shalom** and the **kingdom (reign) of God**. We could call these words or phrases "systemic" because they embody a whole set of values. In the scripture passages we have just read, God's vision for the world clearly embraces safety, plenty, freedom, health and peace.

The verses from Psalm 137 and Jeremiah 29 add another important element. Knowing the context helps you here. Psalm 137 is the outcry of those forceably removed by King Nebuchadnezzar from their beloved Jerusalem to Babylon. Quite frankly, they hated the place. They longed to go home and were outraged that God had permitted them to be deported. "What is God's word to us?" they wanted to know. Jeremiah, the prophet, speaks for God. Picture their shock at what he says:

"'Your Shalom will be found in Babylon's Shalom.' The well-being of the chosen ones is tied to the well-being of that hated metropolis, which the chosen people fear and resent. It is profound and disturbing to discover that this remarkable religious vision will have to be actualized in the civil community."

(*Living Toward a Vision*, Walter Brueggemann,) [Philadelphia, Pa.: United Church Press, 1976], 23)

The temptation is strong to withdraw into our own little world—that of our families, our congregations, our economically-zoned communities. But the biblical injunction is to work toward God's vision for the whole of creation right here, in the middle of our captivity.

Brueggemann continues: "The stuff of well-being is the sordid collection of rulers, soldiers, wardens, and carpetbaggers in Judah and in every other place of displaced, exhausted hope." God's intentions are to be sought in the economic and political issues of today. We are to follow God's vision in every aspect of life. The vision calls us to the "even better." It may be beyond our grasp in any one place or at any one time. But it is important to try to discern God's vision for us, and to develop goals for realizing it in our time.

What kind of exile do we experience? Have we retreated into a neighborhood or community which is racially and/or economically exclusive? Might we lose our jobs? Are we becoming more alienated from the political process? What else makes you feel separated from others and the life you want?

What visions inspire you today? Think of examples from close around you and from places far from home—among the nations of the South, in the new nations of Eastern Europe, among indigenous peoples in the Americas. What are the elements of a vision which sustains you?

JONES, YOU'VE ONLY GOT A MASTER'S DEGREE IN BUSINESS, WHEN YOU GET A PH.D, THEN YOU CAN DRY TOO!

TRY THIS EXERCISE: *Group 2*

Then God said "Let there be light;" and there was light. And God saw that the light was good . . . God called the dry land Earth, and the waters that were gathered together God called Seas. And God saw that it was good . . . The earth brought forth vegetation; plants yielding seed of every kind, and trees of every kind bearing fruit with the seed in it. And God saw that it was good . . . God made the two great lights—the greater to rule the day and the lesser light to rule the night—and the stars. God set them in the dome of the sky to give light upon the earth to rule over the day and over the night, and to separate the light from the darkness. And God saw that it was good. . . So God created the great sea monsters and every living creature that moves, of every kind, with which the waters swarm, and every winged bird of every kind. And God saw that it was good. . . God made the wild animals of every kind, and the cattle of every kind, and everything that creeps along the ground of every kind. And God saw that it was good. . . So God created humankind in his image, in the image of God they were created . . . God saw everything that had been made, and indeed it was very good. (Gen. 1)

* * *

For God so loved the world that he gave his only Son, so that everyone who believes in him may not perish but have eternal life. (John 3:16)

We know love by this, that he laid down his life for us—and we ought to lay down our lives for one another. (I John 3:16)

* * *

"Not everyone who says to me, 'Lord, Lord,' will enter the kingdom of heaven, but only the one who does the will of my Father who is in heaven." (Matt. 7:21)

Take away from me the noise of your songs; I will not listen to the melody of your harps. But let justice roll down like waters, and righteousness like an everflowing stream. (Amos 5:23-24)

* * *

"Do not store up for yourselves treasures on earth, where moth and rust consume and where thieves break in and steal; but store up for yourselves treasures in heaven, where neither moth nor rust consumes and where thieves do not break in and steal. For where your treasure is, there your heart will be also." (Matt. 6:19-21)

These Scriptures underline the biblical insistence that spiritual and material matters are inextricably linked.

A church worker in Swaziland tells the story of LaNdwande, a thirty-year-old woman who illustrates this merging of the spiritual and material aspects of life:

"LaNdwande has a liberated husband by Swazi standards. He allows her to do many things that other Swazi women are not allowed to do. Partly, this is because he is quick to see that what she is doing is bringing more income into the family. Since she first became my assistant, she has helped us in many ways besides with sewing classes. She has helped to organize women's groups in several communities, both for sewing and for handicraft production. She has been involved in organizing water and other projects, including one group that is attempting to raise poultry to sell for meat.

"One day she said to me: 'Now I am free. Before the Council of Churches sent volunteers to work here, I was dependent on my husband for everything. But now I have learned to sew, and I sell children's clothes and get my own money. I have learned how to make the sisal baskets and I can sell them. I have learned how to organize a group and run a meeting. Now we have 10 women who are going to raise and sell poultry together. I have learned how to go to the government offices and talk to the officers and ask for their help. So now I am free. My husband is getting to be an old man. If he should die, I will have no worries because now I know I can make it on my own. My children won't suffer, because I can take care of them and send them to school. I will not have to depend on my husband's brother, nor will I have to obey his family.

What common theme do you see in these passages?

★

I am free.'"

(From 1990 newsletter of the Division of Overseas Ministries, Disciples of Christ, by Bill and Linda Weeks Watson)

To know that you are free is a profoundly spiritual insight; to know how to make baskets, sell poultry and talk to government officials are very earthy activities. LaNdwande has understood the biblical vision correctly—material and spiritual belong together.

Unlike some of the other cultures which surrounded them, the Hebrews believed that spirit and matter are united. A major difference between the Bible's story of creation and that of other religions is that God views the created physical world as good. The central event for understanding Jewish history—being set free from slavery in Egypt—is both a physical and a spiritual happening. God constantly reminds Jews of that heritage. Part of their responsibility in the covenant with God was seeing to such practical matters as looking out for the stranger and leaving some grain in the field for the hungry. (Deut. 5:12-15; 10:17-19; 24:21-22)

It is intriguing that the verse many Christians learned as children, John 3:16, is echoed in I John 3:16 but with the added implication that God's gift of the Son to us is to be matched with our willingness to die for our neighbor.

The parable of the courtroom (Matthew 25:31-46), in which the "nations" are brought to trial, states the principle in its bluntest form. To paraphrase only slightly,

"Your spiritual affirmation that I am Lord means nothing. Go feed the hungry, welcome the stranger, visit the sick and those in jail." How plain can it be!

But this emphasis on living out our faith in the real world in concrete, reconciling acts should not cause us to slip into the false assumption that salvation comes through our good works. Even as we feed the hungry, we affirm that one cannot live by bread alone. We rightly speak a word of judgment, beginning with ourselves, to a culture in which shopping at the mall is a favorite form of recreation, and in which millions of dollars and some of the most creative minds of our time are wasted in persuading us that we need more material things. But the Bible insists that the answer is not to spiritualize our faith. A "spiritual life" is one lived in response to the indwelling of the Holy Spirit. So we need to live "spiritually" when we pray and worship and love, but also when we play and work and spend.

The last passage clearly does not mean that we should not have savings accounts nor take out insurance policies. But it does emphasize that the meaning of life is not to be found in the accumulation of things but in our search for the will of God for our lives.

What experiences have you had that demonstrate that the spiritual and physical aspects of life are tied together? What is spiritual about feeding the hungry? What is physical about loving God?

PALOMO
LA JORNADA
Mexico City
MEXICO

Cartoonists & Writers Syndicate

TRY THIS EXERCISE: *Group 3*

And Jesus said, "Truly I tell you, no prophet is accepted in the prophet's hometown. But the truth is, there were many widows in Israel in the time of Elijah, when the heaven was shut up three years and six months, and there was a severe famine all over the land; yet Elijah was sent to none of them except to a widow at Zareth in Sidon. There were also many lepers in Israel in the time of the prophet Elisha, and none was cleansed except Naaman the Syrian." (Luke 4: 24-27)

* * *

There is no longer Jew or Greek, there is no longer slave or free, there is no longer male or female; for all of you are one in Christ Jesus. (Gal. 3:28)

If your enemies are hungry, give them bread to eat; if they are thirsty, give them water to drink." (Prov. 25:21)

* * *

Peter went up on the roof to pray . . . He saw the heaven opened and something like a large sheet coming down . . . In it were all kinds of four-footed creatures and reptiles and birds of the air. Then he heard a voice saying, "Get up, Peter, kill and eat." But Peter said, "By no means, Lord; for I have never eaten anything that is profane or unclean." The voice said to him again, a second time, "What God has made clean, you must not call profane."

* * *

The following day they came to Caesarea. Cornelius was expecting them. . . And as Peter talked with him, he went in and found that many had assembled; and Peter said to them, "You yourselves know that it is unlawful for a Jew to associate with or to visit a Gentile; but God has shown me that I should not call anyone profane or unclean." (Acts 10)

What teaching is common to these passages?

★

These passages help us to recognize that the community of which we are a part is a worldwide family. The barriers which seem to separate us are overcome in Jesus Christ.

The story of Peter and Cornelius in Acts 10 makes this point powerfully. Peter's religious training had taught him how to separate foods and people into categories—clean/unclean, good/bad, blessed/cursed by God. So it is not surprising that when told in a dream to eat food he understood to be unclean, he refused. Then came the new teaching: "What God has made clean, you must not call profane."

Peter was bright enough to know that the voice wasn't talking about food alone. When he followed the servants of Cornelius, a Gentile, to Caesarea, Peter was practicing what we would call "civil disobedience." He had learned the lesson well. God shows no partiality.

Jesus makes the same point in the synagogue at Bethlehem (Luke 4:24-27). The radical nature of Jesus' teaching about Elijah visiting the widow in Sidon cannot be seen unless we understand the context. To update, imagine that you are being told about Americans offering free health care in Cuba, education in Libya, or wheat in the former Soviet Union.

"The most staggering expression of the [biblical] vision is that all persons are children of a single family, members of a single tribe, heirs of a single hope, and bearers of a single destiny, namely the care and the management of all of God's creation." (Brueggemann, *Living Toward a Vision*, p. 15)

When we learn that some Mexican workers labor in unsafe conditions at low wages in border factories which export their goods to Canada and the United States, what do we feel? Should we consider the plight of maquila-doras workers as a family crisis?

But there are family celebrations too. We can rejoice with Asoke and Shali. Only a few years ago, this couple in rural India was destitute. They moved to Calcutta where they lived on the streets. Wth her two children, Shali picked over trash piles and garbage for items to sell for a few rupees. She did not think about a better life; this was her fate, her karma. Asoke pushed a two-wheeled cart delivering goods throughout the city.

One day a stranger spoke with Shali and asked if she would like to learn to sew. She was a quick learner. The church-sponsored Development Center then helped her get a small business loan, buy a sewing machine, open a bank account and make payments. Every step was a struggle to convince her husband that such initiative on the part of a woman was appropriate. But when her income made it possible for Asoke to buy his own cart, thus tripling his income, all opposition ceased. Shali and Asoke and their children have moved to a shack in a squatter's colony and are saving for the down payment on a government apartment. Now that's something for us as family members to celebrate!

What experiences have broadened your sense of family? What are the chief barriers to seeing others as members of God's family? What celebrations and what crises are occurring today in our wider family?

EARTH
DAY
1992

Cartoonists & Writers Syndicate

SHUTO
LA REPUBBLICA
Rome
ITALY

TRY THIS EXERCISE: *Group 4*

You shall make this response before the Lord your God: "A wandering Aramean was my ancestor; he went down into Egypt and lived there as an alien, few in number, and there he became a great nation, mighty and populous. When the Egyptians treated us harshly and afflicted us, by imposing hard labor on us, we cried to the Lord, the God of our ancestors; the Lord heard our voice and saw our affliction, our toil, and our oppression. The Lord brought us out of Egypt with a mighty hand and an outstretched arm, with a terrifying display of power, and with signs and wonders; and he brought us into this place and gave us this land, a land flowing with milk and honey. . . ." (Deut. 26:5-9)

* * *

Indeed, the body does not consist of one member but of many. If the foot would say, "Because I am not a hand, I do not belong to the body," that would not make it any less a part of the body. And if the ear would say, "Because I am not an eye, I do not belong to the body," that would not make it any less a part of the body. If the whole body were an eye, where would the hearing be? If the whole body were hearing, where would the sense of smell be? But as it is, God arranged the members in the body, each one of them, as he chose. If all were a single member, where would the body be? As it is, there are many members, yet one body. The eye cannot say to the hand, "I have no need of you," nor the head to the feet, I have no need of you." (I Cor. 12:14-21)

* * *

"Tell us, then, what you think. Is it lawful to pay taxes to the emperor, or not?" But Jesus, aware of their malice, said, "Why are you putting me to the test, you hypocrites? Show me the coin used for the tax." And they brought him a denarius. Then he said to them, "Whose head is this, and whose title?" They answered, "The emperor's." Then he said to them, "Give therefore to the emperor the things that are the emperor's, and to God the things that are God's." (Matt. 22:17-21)

Paul states it clearly in the letter to the Corinthians: Not "I" but "we," not "one" but "many." Sometimes we miss the humor in the Bible. Just imagine a huge ear walking down the street pretending it didn't need to see or smell or talk!

When our children were growing up, we would sometimes pause before a meal not only to bless the hands that prepared it but also to remind ourselves of all the individuals who had helped bring the food to our table—farmers, road builders, those who make fertilizers and trucks and tractors, members of the Teamster's Union, owners of clothing stores, workers at the supermarket, bank employees, manufacturers of kitchenware—and on and on.

The passage from Deuteronomy is a concise summary of the identity of the Jewish people. The shift in pronouns is intriguing. Slavery in Egypt changed "he" to "we." From then on, the biblical emphasis is on a people, a community. God's covenant is with a community of believers.

In some silent-meeting Quaker communities, before a member can be married in the church, the couple must meet with the elders for advice and counsel, to determine whether the marriage is appropriate.

How many of us seek the advice of other church members before making important life decisions? If we are trying to change our spending patterns, do we bring our cancelled checks to a church group for discussion? Before we cast a ballot for a political candidate who may vote matters affecting millions

What "pointer" do you find in these passages?

★

of God's people, do we check our criteria for judgment with other Christians? Yet living in community seems to be the biblical emphasis.

The "render unto Caesar" passage is an excellent example of the biblical tendency to provide principles by which to live rather than rules which give precise guidance for every situation. This teaching also makes clear that we live in various communities and have differing responsibilities to them. We may well differ in our understanding of the power which the state should have over our lives (taxation? abortion? prayer in public schools?), but it is clear that from the Christian perspective, the state can never be given our total commitment.

Robert Bellah and his associates argue in their books *Habits of the Heart* and *The Good Society* that our failure to solve some of the critical social problems of our time is due in large part to an over-emphasis on individualism. For those in the Judeo-Christian tradition, however, the faith community must provide the context within which our individual decisions are made.

This biblical pointer has major implications for global economics.

If we accept that we are all members of the worldwide family of God, that we are individuals-in-community, then whether we are citizens of Canada or the United States we must listen with openness when citizens of the "Third World" charge that our spending decisions as individuals and as nations are dooming them to ongoing misery.

For some time, church leaders throughout the world have been wrestling with a power question: Who should decide how the churches' resources for global outreach should be spent? Should the decisions be made only by those who "give" the funds? Or should those on the receiving end have a favored seat at the table?

Do the resources belong to one, or all?

Think of some examples of individualism and cooperation in the lifestyles practiced in Canada and the United States. Which of these qualities are emphasized in our work situations? What might cause a Christian to take a stand in opposition to a community rather than standing with it?

TRY THIS EXERCISE: *Group 5*

When you reap the harvest of your land, you shall not reap to the very edges of your field, or gather the gleanings of your harvest; you shall leave them for the poor and for the alien: I am the Lord your God. (Lev. 23:22)

* * *

"He has shown strength with his arm; he has scattered the proud in the thoughts of their hearts. He has brought down the powerful from their thrones, and lifted up the lowly; he has filled the hungry with good things, and sent the rich away empty." (Luke 1:51-53)

* * *

When he came to Nazareth, where he had been brought up, he went to the synagogue on the sabbath day, as was his custom. He stood up to read, and the scroll of the prophet Isaiah was given to him. He unrolled the scroll and found the place where it was written: "The Spirit of the Lord is upon me, because he has anointed me to bring good news to the poor. He has sent me to proclaim release to the captives, and recovery of sight to the blind, to let the oppressed go free, to proclaim the year of the Lord's favor." (Luke 4:16-19)

What is the message of these Scriptures?

★

One biblical "pointer" from these passages goes to the heart of our study of global economics. Time and time again in the Bible, the mandate for action is—care for the widows and orphans (including representing them before the authorities), feed the hungry, look after the stranger in your midst, do justice, show mercy.

We need have no doubt on this matter. Woe to those who lie between satin sheets, thunders Amos. Woe to those who overcharge the poor of my people, proclaims Isaiah. In a parable, Jesus consigns the wealthy man to hell because he ignores a beggar at his gate (Luke 16:19-23). The nations brought to judgment are likewise sentenced for their failure to minister to the poor (Matt. 25:41-43).

It is said that during medieval times, when the Magnificat was read during the Christmas Eve service in the great cathedrals, the serfs would stand and cheer. They knew good news when they heard it!

Does this emphasis on God's special concern for the poor contradict the gospel's claim that each one of us is loved by God? Not at all. No parent should have any trouble understanding the biblical perspective. Parents love all their children but recognize that sometimes one child needs extra attention, extra caring and love and help.

How do you feel about a "preferential option for the poor?"

Some would say bluntly that a church which demonstrates no

concern for the poor is not altogether a church. What do you think? Why?

A visitor attended Mass at the Mother House of Mother Teresa's Missionary Sisters of Charity in Calcutta. Reflecting upon that experience, she wrote: "These women have nothing and yet they have everything. They are at peace. They are filled with joy. They love life because life has meaning, and they are connected to others. They are so simple and yet so rich. . . It is not a duty to help the poor; it is a privilege." (*Ministry of Money* newsletter, December 1990, p. 5)

For Christians to fail to respond

to the cries of the poor—whether as individuals or corporately as a church—is to deny the Christ we profess to serve.

If we ourselves are not economically poor, what relationship should we have with those who are? What are some Biblical examples of a charitable approach? What are some Biblical examples of a justice approach? Why is it more comfortable for many middle class Christians to offer charity but not work for justice? What does it mean to work for justice today? Is the Bible concerned about economic poverty, or only spiritual poverty?

"One more billion—and I swear I will go gentle into that good night!"

Drawing by Ed Fisher, © 1991 by The Christian Century. Reprinted by permission of Ed Fisher.

TRY THIS EXERCISE: *Group 6*

Cain said to his brother Abel, "Let us go out to the field." And when they were in the field, Cain rose up against his brother Abel, and killed him. Then the Lord said to Cain, "Where is your brother Abel?" He said, "I do not know; am I my brother's keeper?" (Gen. 4:8-9)

* * *

All have sinned and fall short of the glory of God. . . . For I do not do the good I want, but the evil I do not want is what I do. (Rom. 3:23, 7:19)

Bless the Lord, O my soul, and all that is within me, bless his holy name. Bless the Lord, O my soul, and do not forget all his benefits—who forgives all your iniquity. (Ps. 103:1-3a)

* * *

If we say we have no sin, we deceive ourselves, and the truth is not in us. If we confess our sins, he who is faithful and just will forgive us our sins and cleanse us from all unrighteousness. (I John 1:8-9)

* * *

But his master replied, "You wicked and lazy slave! You knew, did you, that I reap where I did not sow, and gather where I did not scatter? Then you ought to have invested my money with the bankers, and on my return I would have received what was my own with interest. So take the talent from him, and give it to the one with the talents. For to all those who have, more will be given, and they will have an abundance; but from those who have nothing, even what they have will be taken away." (Matt. 25:26-29)

What does the Bible say about sin and forgiveness?

Christians have discussed "original sin" for centuries. Much energy has been wasted arguing whether snakes or women or men or God caused the problem. Adam's sin of self-seeking and self-centeredness has passed through every generation. We have learned one thing: "All have sinned and fall short of the glory of God."

Like Paul, we can look at ourselves, then observe those around us, and realize that although human beings have a real tendency to act in self-centered ways, they also have the capacity to rise above their self-centeredness.

Can anyone read about the enslavement, cruel transport and humiliating treatment of African people—or see racism at work today—and pretend that sin isn't an issue? As we learn more about the decimation of the indigenous people of the Americas, whether at the hands of Spanish conquistadores or American pioneers, can we doubt that sin exists?

Can anyone reflect on the Holocaust and doubt the fact of sin? Can anyone remember the massacre of the Kampuchean people by Pol Pot's Khmer Rouge and not ache over our inhumanity to each other? Can anyone of us review our own lifestyle decisions and and not lament, "I do not do the good I want?"

But the gospel does not leave us in guilt and despair. The good news is that sin is not the last word. We are called to new life; that is the good news!

★

As Christians we believe that through Jesus Christ we are forgiven by God. We are accepted. As theologian Paul Tillich put it, "Accept the fact that you are accepted."

"If we confess our sins, God is faithful and just to forgive." We are no longer bound up by guilt. We need not be limited to our past commitments nor to our present actions or inactions. With the forgiveness of God, we can start over. Those who have experienced forgiveness do rise above the too common self-centeredness of human nature.

Have we not stood in awe of people like Cardinal Paul Emile Leger who resigned as archbishop of Montreal to establish a mission hospital in Cameroon? He once said, "I am at my best when helping the most neglected people of the Third World—the lepers, the crippled, the physically and mentally ill, the orphans."

Do not the lives of Fannie Lou Hamer, a powerful leader of the civil rights movement in the United States in the 1960s, or Dorothy Day, Roman Catholic "saint" and friend of the poor, motivate us to less self-centered living? Have we not known persons who have placed the welfare of others above their own? Have we not known others who have seen across the artificial barriers of class, race, gender and/or nationality and worked together with others for a common good? And have not each of us, on occasion, remembering the faith we profess, put our fears or prejudices

aside and reached out to others?

Our understanding and interpretation of human behavior affects the kind of society we construct, the kind of economy we have. Our system of laws, policies, regulations, and private and public institutions is based on certain assumptions. They act as carrots and sticks to encourage and punish individual and collective behavior. Some economic policies encourage consumptive and acquisitive behavior. Some encourage competition; others cooperation. Some laws say certain things are best left in the public domain for the greater good of all (e.g. public parks and schools), rather than be determined by individual wishes. Others do the opposite. What do you think about our basic nature? Are we "good," "bad," "selfish," "altruistic," "competitive," "cooperative?" Can you identify some of the assumptions embodied in economic policy and laws?

In the parable of the talents, if verse 29 were to be taken literally, Jesus would appear to be saying that the wealthy will have additional rewards and the poor will be made even more destitute. That would be in contrast to many other of Jesus' teachings. The passage must deal with one aspect of our self-centeredness, our "sin." We are not to avoid our responsibilities, especially those we are convinced are God-given.

It is intriguing to think of slight variations in some of the parables. Suppose the two-talent person had come to the master reporting that

he had given his talents away to those who were hungry and homeless. Would such a use of his talents have been unacceptable? It seems unlikely in light of the parable which immediately follows (verses 31-46), with its teaching of feeding the hungry and clothing the naked. But any attempt to "play it safe" or not to risk is rejected in this parable.

Is forgiveness possible without repentance and a desire to make restitution? Does sin consist sometimes not of self-centeredness but of failing to use our strengths to confront injustice? Should we think more about the goodness of human nature than about its limitations?

Here's one way of stating the teachings from these biblical passages:

1. **God has a vision of wholeness, of well-being for creation.**

2. **The spiritual and material aspects of life are inextricably linked.**

3. **We are part of God's world-wide family.**

4. **We live as individuals but have responsibility to the community.**

5. **We are meant to have a special concern for the poor and the powerless.**

6. **We are self-centered but have capacity for generosity; we are forgiven; we can try again.**

Just owning a compass that gives us a true direction will not get us to our destination. We need more precise guidance. Whether we are deciding how to spend our own money, or participating in building a congregation's budget, or deciding how we will respond to our government's economic policies toward other countries, we need to know how to move from our Biblical "pointers" to more specific helps. Let us begin with ethical thinking.

© 1991 NORMAN LOG

How Do Christians Reach Decisions?

Christian ethics involves careful thinking about how our Christian faith commitments can be translated into life decisions about what is right and wrong.

The ancient Greeks, who thought a lot about ethics, felt that in any ethical decision or act, you had to examine
1) your motive,
2) your goal,
3) your means of achieving your goal,
4) the likely results of your proposed action.

Suppose you are walking with a friend on a city street and someone approaches you and asks for money to buy food. As you try to decide what to do, the Greeks would have you consider:

1. Your motive. Do you want to give the money in order to:
— help someone in need
— impress your friend with your generosity
— follow what you believe Jesus would do
— make yourself feel good

Or, do you *not* want to give, because responding to begging
— encourages laziness
— fosters dependency
— doesn't solve the root cause of poverty
— is foolish when the money will go for alcohol anyway

2. Your goal. What do you expect to accomplish with the action you choose to take? Look at the choices above, and analyze what might be accomplished with action according to each motive.

3. Your method. How do you intend to accomplish your goal?

Maybe you don't want to give money, but you don't want the person to go hungry, either. You might:
— give the person your phone number and say that you have some work that needs to be done
— tell the person that you will be at the same place tomorrow and will help him find a job
— take him to a multi-service center for help

Maybe you don't want to give money, because you don't believe it will be used for food. You might:
— give him a lecture about the evils of alcoholism
— offer to buy a sandwich and a cup of coffee
— shake your head and walk on by

4. Results. What is likely to happen as a result of your action? The decision has an impact not only on the person who asks for help, but also on you, and on the friend who sees what you do.

GABLE
Globe and Mail
Toronto
CANADA

Even though we tell ourselves we shouldn't have to think this hard before we give a dollar, much of the above probably runs through our minds at the moment of such encounters. And we probably want to be honest with ourselves about how we are feeling, while we are thinking about what to do! We tend to be critical of those who do "good" deeds for "bad" reasons, for example, the person who gives generously in order to win the plaudits of others or the person who prays fervently in order to be thought of as pious. (Matthew 6:5)

To the extent that we think carefully about decisions that involve ethical choices, we do have a goal in mind and some idea of how to reach it. But perhaps we are not always as insightful as we should be about possible results of our actions. Or maybe it isn't insight that we lack, but information.

Sometimes we may have a clear idea of what is right (or wrong), and it's easy to know how to act. Other times the decision does not seem clear—one action could have different results, or there are many different possible courses of action, or even inaction could produce different results!

"Doing something" about global economics is a bit more complicated than "doing something" about the man on the street, obviously. Does that mean we shake our heads and say, "It's too much for me?" No!

We still have to find a way of translating our Christian faith into action. We have to find ways of putting our biblical assumptions to work in the world.

STILL ANOTHER EXERCISE

Consider the following situation. Then write down what you think this couple should do and why.

John and Mary have two children and a combined family income of $60,000. They are both professional musicians but about 40 percent of their income comes in direct cash payments from students for lessons. John and Mary are active church members. When they fill out their income tax forms, they must declare all of their income. But they know that it would be almost impossible for the government to find out how much income they receive from students, and thus, they could cheat on the figure.

What should they do?

Most of us will say that they should not cheat! After all, there are certain rules for Christian living and being honest is one of them. A rule tells you precisely what to do when faced with a situation of right and wrong.

Even though we know what is right, we may be tempted to cheat, for "good" reasons as well as "bad." We may say we can put the money to better use than the government (helping the poor vs. buying missiles). But there are ways to make a statement about government use of money without violating our code of ethics.

For Christians, rules may come directly from one's study of the Bible, from a particular Christian community, from a claimed personal revelation, or from a conscience informed by Scripture, Christian tradition, reason, and experience.

One of the first children studied by Harvard psychiatrist Robert Coles was Ruby Bridges, the six-year-old who helped integrate the public schools of New Orleans in 1960. For months, twice a day, Ruby and three other African-American children, protected by federal marshals, walked through lines of adults screaming threats and profanity at them.

Coles discovered that every day as she walked through this angry mob, Ruby would pause and offer a prayer for them.

He was amazed that any six-year-old could do this, and he talked to Ruby about it on several occasions.

"Ruby, you know, I'm still puzzled about this. I'm trying to figure out why you think you

★

should be the one to pray for such people, given what they do to you twice a day, five days a week." Ruby answered, "Well, especially it should be me." She went on to say that Jesus went through a lot of trouble and he said about the people who were causing this trouble, "Forgive them, because they don't know what they're doing."

Ruby had a rule, learned in her family and in church, rooted in the teachings of Jesus. She didn't have to wonder what was right or wrong. ("Immanence and Transcendence," Robert Coles, in the *Princeton Seminary Bulletin*, 1984, p. 203 ff)

We all need rules to live by, for some ethical dilemmas can be solved by following such rules. What rules do you find valuable for conducting your life today? Sometimes, though, we find ourselves facing a dilemma when conflicting rules or values come into play. Can you offer some economic examples from your own life? From current events?

If we think that the Ten Commandments in Exodus 20 are good rules to follow, on what grounds do we reject the clear rule in Exodus 21 that masters may beat their slaves as long as they don't kill them?! Some Christians stand outside clinics where abortion is offered as an option with placards announcing the rule, "Thou shalt not kill!" Other Christians enthusiastically support military excursions in which thousands of persons (including many children), are killed.

What rules for living today have you found in the Bible?

ANOTHER SITUATION

Peggy Northrup is an engineer working for a major corporation. The company makes an essential part of the firing mechanism for nuclear weapons. As a Christian, Peggy is concerned about peace issues and she wonders if she should find a different job. She prays long and hard about the situation. She decides that she will stay in her job, because she believes that in the real world, peace comes from being strong enough to deter any other nation from attacking you.

Because Peggy prayed about her decision, does that mean she made the right choice for her? If not, how does prayer help us to decide between right and wrong?

★

Most Christians will agree that prayer is an essential part of deciding right and wrong. But we must be wary of using prayer as a way of assuring ourselves that God approves of what we have already decided—what we want, or what's easy! When we pray, we may not hear God speaking in a literal way. But if we are centered on God as the source of those values that we believe to be ultimate and universal, and are open to new insights and possibilities for the questions at hand, then prayer becomes a transforming way of reaching ethical decisions.

Unfortunately we all have read of bizarre situations in which individuals claim that God told them to do every kind of murder and mayhem. Furthermore, equally sincere Christians, praying about identical situations, come out with opposite answers.

Clearly, prayer has other important functions of praise and thanksgiving, of confession and intercession. Can it be used to reach decisions on economic questions? Yes! But prayer alone is not enough. With complex issues, information gathered from research, or opinions gathered from discussion from others, are also required.

Peggy needs to do more than pray. What else should she do?

How do you use prayer when struggling with a difficult decision?

A DIFFERENT SITUATION

A diesel engine company sold a pump to a remote village in India to provide fresh water and better health to the villagers. Later, one of the pump parts needed replacement. The corporation's Indian representative reported that to get the part through customs, a bribe must be paid. He asked corporate headquarters for advice. The corporation's leadership is committed to making decisions in the marketplace from a Christian perspective. What should they recommend and why?

Some ethicists believe that there is little you can know about what you ought to do until you actually have to make a decision in a given situation. Then, the only values to be applied are love of God and neighbors which we must express to the highest degree possible in our decisions and actions. All rules and regulations, all ethical principles and policies must be reexamined when the actual decision is made.

A few years ago, the United States made a grant to a Latin American country. As part of the agreement, a portion of the grant was to be in American wheat. Let us assume that the motives were good. The intent was not only to assist a country in need of help but also to provide assistance to American wheat farmers. However, the imported wheat drove down the price of wheat grown by the local farmers who, unable to make ends meet, shifted to growing coca for the drug trade.

Life constantly presents us with situations in which we must try to love our neighbors. In helping one neighbor, we may be unable to help another. It is common to speak of having to choose the lesser of two evils. But "situational" ethicists would say that to the extent we have tried to make the best response to the supreme value of love, the lesser evil is actually a positive good. Ethicist Joseph Fletcher, who did much to popularize this position, calls the approach "love using its head."

Situationalists, of course, understand that the word "love" can refer to different realities and values. They distinguish between a self-centered love, a love that includes both the self and others, and an *agape* love that is centered in a concern for the welfare of the other and is found in its fullest

★

sense only in the love of God.

In the India exercise above, one would have to ask such questions as, "Is the health and well-being of the villagers more important than a rule about not paying bribes?" (Is this a parallel to Jesus healing on the sabbath?) Or does bribery so destroy the possibility of building community that it must be rejected in every situation?

One hazard of situational ethics is the temptation to make the rules fit the occasion, and to consider all ethical choices equally valid. Lying is all right in this situation; cheating is okay in that. However, if we do not do some advance thinking, we may not be able to make the appropriate ethical choice when it is required.

The situationalists say it's dangerous to offer a simplistic moral code for a complicated world, and they're probably right. Repeated surveys yield the discouraging report that the ethical conduct of church-goers differs little from that of the rest of the population. Possibly we Christians have made it appear that living a faithful Christian life is a fairly simple business and have failed to discuss the complexities of many contemporary world situations in our congregations.

Most of us would prefer more guidance for making ethical decisions than the situationalists offer. But we should remember that ethical codes established apart from real life situations may not always help us, either.

In what kinds of decisions do you think situational ethics would be most helpful? Least helpful?

YET ANOTHER SITUATION

Alice has been a Congresswoman for several terms. Although she agrees that she must represent the views of her many different constituents, as a Christian she is also committed to trying to reach decisions that reflect her faith. During this session of Congress she must help advise the U.S. representatives to the International Monetary Fund about what conditions the Fund will set for Mexico and Brazil before refinancing their large foreign debt. What information will Alice need as she weighs the factors and tries to make a responsible, Christian, ethical decision? How will Christian faith help her to think through this issue? What Biblical pointers can she use?

Put down your ideas.

★

To the rescue: middle axioms

Wouldn't it be helpful if we could find some ethical guidance that was
   a) not as rigid as a rule,
   b) open to discussion as well as prayer,
   c) more widely applicable than decisions related to single situations.

Such guidance does exist!

   A system of ethical thinking using *middle axioms* applies principles that
lie between our basic theological convictions (our biblical "pointers"), and
the complicating factors of the actual situation.

   A faith community agrees on these principles as ethically binding
until the group decides that they should be changed in light of new
Christian understandings. For example, a middle axiom which might
come from belief in the worldwide family of God is that "forced racial
segregation is wrong."

   A middle axiom is not a rule and does not tell us exactly what to do
on every occasion. Rather, it is a yardstick to help us measure the rightness or wrongness of a decision. Middle axioms fall in the middle of a
three-step process of making decisions.

Step 1: What are my faith positions (or those of my church), on what is
         ultimately good and true?
Step 2: What middle axiom(s) can be drawn from these?
Step 3: How do these apply in this specific situation?

EXAMPLE:

Suppose we wish to develop goals for any economic system, national or
global. A three-step process for one goal might begin like this:

Step 1: One of our Biblical "pointers" is that we live in community, not
         only with our wordwide neighbors but also with the whole
         created universe.

Step 2: A middle axiom is that an economic system should not support a
         technology or practice that unduly pollutes the atmosphere or
         wastes the earth's resources.

Step 3: Apply these principles to decisions about regulating the disposal
         of industrial waste.

This approach is not, of course, a "Three Simple Steps To Mastering All
Ethical Dilemmas." But it is a helpful way of moving from what may
seem to be abstractly stated faith positions to practical, specific applications.

Let's see how we might apply certain middle axioms to the six biblical pointers developed previously, and address current situations or issues in global economics.

Group 1

Biblical pointer:	God has a vision of wholeness, of well-being for Creation.
Middle axiom:	No economic system should be identified with the reign of God.
Current issues:	Free market capitalism, deregulation, environmental regulation, gambling.

Group 2

Biblical pointer:	The spiritual and material aspects of life are inextricably linked.
Middle axiom:	An economic system should make it possible for all persons to meet their needs for food, clothing, housing, and health.
Current issues:	Minimum wage, poverty, welfare policies, health delivery systems.

Group 3

Biblical pointer:	We are part of God's worldwide family.
Middle axiom:	An economic system should lessen the gap between luxury and poverty within a nation and among nations.
Current issues:	National tax policies, Third World Debt, international trade practices.

Group 4

Biblical pointer:	We live as individuals in community.
Middle axiom:	An economic system should balance individual freedom with encouragement of cooperative and community-building approaches. An economic system should not pollute the atmosphere nor waste the earth's resources.
Current issues:	Governmental involvement in the economy; work rules; maternity/paternity leaves; cooperatives, credit unions; worker-owned companies; pollution; consumption of luxury goods.

Group 5

Biblical pointer: We are to have a special relationship with the poor and the powerless.

Middle axiom: An economic system should provide an adequate standard of living for all, including those who cannot or should not work outside the home.

Current issues: Welfare policies and practices, housing for low-income people, government training programs.

Group 6

Biblical pointer: We are self-centered but have capacity for generosity and justice; we are forgiven; we can try again.

Middle axiom: An economic system should provide checks and balances to prevent undue concentration of power and provide mechanisms for evaluation and change.

Current issues: Labor-management relations, anti-trust laws, right-to-work statutes, government regulation of commerce and industry.

* * *

Well, where are we?

- We have looked at what is going on in God's world.
- We have examined some biblical teachings.
- We have described several ways to move from these teachings to specific decisions.

Now it is time to turn to global economics.

Can We Make Sense Out of Dollars?

An introduction to economic thinking and some ideas on how the global system works—or doesn't!

Economics has been called the "dismal science" and, unfortunately, many of us have looked at it in that way. But the word comes from the Greek *oikonomos*, meaning "household manager"—and that makes all of us economists! (Interestingly, the root word for house in Greek, *oikos*, is also the root in "ecumenical.")

One reason we may have difficulty with economics is that the dollar amounts involved in most public issues—millions, billions, trillions (or their Canadian equivalents—millions, thousands of millions, millions of millions), are too big to comprehend.

A U.S. Congressman has remarked that if you spend a million here and a million there, "pretty soon, you're talking about real money." Trouble is, many of us can remember when a nickel or a dime was "real money!"

One way to help ourselves deal with "astronomical" dollar amounts is to look at what they will buy in goods and services. We should learn to deal with them almost as easily as with the numbers we juggle in our household budgeting. Then we can deal better with the choices that need to be made.

If you had $1 billion (U.S.), which would you do?

1. Invest it. Even at a modest 5 percent, $1 billion will earn $137,000 per day.
2. Buy one B-2 bomber.
3. Provide safe drinking water and sanitation for 250 million children.

The discipline of economics provides a method for making critical decisions in the global village in which we all live.

While economists often like to quantify reality and put it in terms of equations and models, in fact, economics is not really a "hard" science like biology or mathematics. Our economic lives consist of relationships, trends, and institutions such as banks, companies, pension funds and stock markets. Studying it involves looking at human behavior and power relationships, so it more resembles what we know as the social sciences—psychology, sociology, anthropology and political science.

Moreover, unlike what we think is the "objective" truth of physics or chemistry, economic interpretations are "subjective"—they are not value neutral. We can see this clearly by the existence of many economic schools of thought. Some start with different assumptions about human behavior (neoclassical economics assumes people are basically selfish; political-economic views often assume cooperation). Others start with the same assumptions, but then branch off in their analysis of a key economic event (e.g. Keynesian economics is a branch off the neoclassical tree. It arose when an Englishman, John Maynard Keynes, had a different understanding of the causes of the "Great Depression" in the 1930s.)

But most of us are less interested in where the economy has been than where it's heading. And we quickly realize that economists can only make well-educated guesses, trying to weigh many factors but unable to foresee every eventuality. To better understand these guesses, then, we need to ask what assumptions lie behind them.

When we raise our sights from our family economies to the global economy, we can see how complex the guessing-game becomes. What will be the short-term economic impact of free trade between Canada and the United States? What will be the costs of the pact being extended to Mexico as well? Will there be another major recession in North America in the 1990s? Can countries of the Third World repay the debt which they owe to banks and international agencies without destroying their own economies?

Economic forecasting is not an exact science, but economists can provide information which is necessary for intelligent and ethical decision-making on many issues. They also can help us understand how things are interrelated, how one choice affects others.

Paul Samuelson, Nobel prize-winning economist, warns against leaving economics to the "experts," however. "It takes a thief to catch a thief. One important reason to study economics is that at every fork in your life's road, you will be bombarded by economic arguments . . . It takes knowledge of economics to be able to resist bad economics." (*Indianapolis Star*, 27 September 1991)

Economic Concepts

We can get started by examining the basic economic ideas. Ask yourself two questions:

1. Would you like to have more money to:
- —buy a new stereo or rent a better apartment?
- —purchase health insurance?
- —help someone or support your favorite charity?
- —put in the bank or credit union?
- —invest in stocks or bonds?
- —start or expand a business?

—

2. Would you like to have more time and energy to:
- —work more and earn more money?
- —increase your voluntary activities?
- —spend with your family?
- —learn a new skill?
- —travel?
- —read or think?

—

Did you answer "yes" to any of these questions? Bet you did—and added a few of your own, no doubt! We may not be able to understand why a ballplayer for the Toronto Blue Jays or the Boston Red Sox is upset that he is only getting paid $2.3 million instead of $2.5 million. But we can recognize that all of us have unfulfilled desires. Maybe not for more material things, though—how many of us have exclaimed, "If only our budget would balance!" or, "If only I had more time!" or "If only I had more money to support all the good causes that need it!"

As we look beyond ourselves, we are aware that millions of people on this planet have unfulfilled *needs*—for food, for shelter, for medical care, for education.

Earlier we compared economics to household management. On a global scale, it seems that people's needs and wants are so great that they can never be met by the resources available. For the economist, scarcity of resources does not mean that a bad frost has caused a shortage of oranges this season. Nor even that we are eliminating many species of birds and plants, thus creating a permanent scarcity. In economics, scarcity of resources means that there is no way to satisfy everyone's wants and therefore choices must be made.

Global economics involves the management of the world's resources—money, land and natural resources, humans, and things made by humans.

Management means making choices about how to use what we have to get what we want. As societies as well as individuals, we have to decide, "What will we make or do? How? For whom?"

Another question: If you had $200 more income per month, what would you do with it?
- —buy a better car?
- —increase your church pledge?
- —eat out more often?
- —start a college education fund for your two-year-old?
- —move to a safer neigborhood?

Economists point out the obvious but often overlooked fact that if you use the $200 to start that college fund, you cannot use it to buy a better car or give it to the church. The real cost of establishing the fund is what you have to sacrifice to do it—eating out more, a better car, a higher church pledge. Economists call this the *"opportunity cost"* of your decision.

Opportunity costs have wide and important implications. The opportunity cost of reading this book is that you cannot use the time for some other worthwhile activity. A congregation that erects a new building cannot use that same money to create an emergency fund for disaster relief efforts. The opportunity cost of a nation's payment of interest on its debt is less money for needed roads or better health care.

Weighing opportunity costs enables you to evaluate whether your decisions:

1) reflect the values by which you live

2) move you toward the goals you are seeking.

★

Opportunity costs are reflected in the saying, "There's no such thing as a free lunch!" When a decision is made to use resources—money, time, energy—there is a cost. And that cost is what has to be given up to implement the decision.

Suppose after setting up your two-year-old's college fund, you learn that you are to receive yet another $200 per month. Assuming that you are a one-child family, would you set up a second college fund? Unlikely. You'd probably examine your other priorities. To a person who is barefoot, a pair of shoes would have high priority. But a person who already owns six pairs of shoes would put little value on another pair, and would not consider such a purchase a

priority. Economists tend to concentrate on what happens if a little more or a little less is bought or sold. They speak of this as decisions *"at the margin."*

You can see several of these economic concepts clearly as you develop a family budget.

Let's look at the Smith family. Mr. and Mrs. Smith have three children, aged 2, 11, and 14, and an after-tax income of $25,000. They are increasingly frustrated because their money decisions do not seem to reflect what they really want to do. They face an apparent scarcity of resources to meet their wants.

They recognize that it is budget-building time. That in itself is an important economic decision. They realize that there is no automatic

pilot that will guide their spending habits in ways that satisfy them. Thoughtful choices must be made based on family values and goals. Not everything can be achieved; opportunity costs must be considered.

They quickly establish that their fixed costs are $6,000 per year for housing and $5,000 for food. That leaves them $14,000. They make a list of other spending categories— clothing, recreation, automobile costs, savings, charitable contributions, medical costs including insurance. (Your list may look different.)

The Smiths see value in all these areas, but haven't thought much about their relative worth. They must start making decisions "at the margin." One thousand dollars will be needed to cover the deductible on health insurance. With three children, this rates highly in their budget priorities, and the decision is easy. After allocating money for other essentials, they ponder personal savings vs. outreach to others. Should they set aside $2,500 for contributions or give less away and put more into the bank?

Economics gives no guidance on what the right decisions are. But the Smiths' understanding of Christian responsibilities will help them make certain decisions on their use of money, and their understanding of economic concepts will help them to see the true costs as they develop their family budget.

How do you spend your disposable (after-tax) income?

Food

Housing

Health insurance

Clothing

Automobile/transportation

Recreation

Contributions

Medical/dental

Savings

Other

While national and global economic decision-making is obviously more complicated, the process does not differ greatly. To find a few million dollars to inoculate the world's children against preventable diseases, what must we do without? That's opportunity cost. If you have 1,000 nuclear warheads, what is the value of one more? That's a decision "at the margin." Some knowledge of economics will equip us to ask those critical questions.

Economic Systems

For Robinson Crusoe, a society of one, economic decisions were straightforward and simple. In very small societies, people may be able to get what they need or want by trading goods or services that other people want. But very soon some kind of money exchange is required, to make up for a lack of desirable resources to trade.

Economists often illustrate this by asking us to imagine that a cruise ship has run aground on a deserted tropical island far off the normal shipping routes. When the passengers realize they are not going to be rescued quickly, they begin to organize their society.

Since Edith is a contractor, she agrees to train a few people and build simple grass houses for everyone. Jeff is a school teacher and is put in charge of a small group responsible for child care. Doris and Henry owned a grocery store, so they agree to lead the search for fruits and nuts. Art has always been an enthusiastic fisherman and gladly agrees to be in charge of that activity.

For a while all goes well. They operate their island economy by a barter system. For providing the service of child care while parents are busy with other tasks, Jeff's group receives food and shelter. Edith's group of builders trades houses for food and child care. But as time passes, life gets more complicated.

Jeff wants to add fish to his fruit-and-nuts diet but no members of Art's fishing group have children. There is no basis for trade. In a perfect world, everyone might give without thought of return, but human nature is seldom like that. The little community soon recognizes the need for a monetary system. Everyone can be paid for their work. Whether goods and services are purchased with money or coconut shells doesn't make any difference. What does matter, though, is the relative value of what people want or need to "buy."

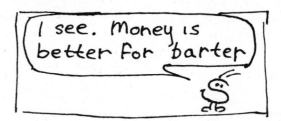

Can you imagine a modern economy trying to operate by the barter system? Have you ever traded goods or services for something you wanted (other than money)?

Systems of exchange are inevitable. And whether they function for 50 people on a desert island, for 30 million in ten provinces, for 240 million in fifty states, or for more than five billion people in the world, economic systems must answer a series of questions:

1. What resources are available?

2. What goods and services shall be produced?

3. How shall they be produced?

4. How shall these goods and services be distributed?

5. How will the answers to Questions 1, 2, 3 and 4 be determined?

Obviously, a number of factors will determine the answers to these questions. Different countries boast different resources. Different societies need or want different goods and services. The means of production vary widely in different parts of the world. Distribution of goods and services depends not only on available means of transport but also on class divisions and other factors.

Let us look briefly at three basic types of economies—traditional, command and market.

Traditional Systems

In trying to determine the answers to the first four questions on the previous page, some societies might ask, simply, "How has it been done before?"

The role of tradition is easy to identify in an earlier age, or a simpler society. What occupation will you follow? Shoemaker. Why? My father was a shoemaker, of course. How do you cut the grain? With a sickle. Why? That's the way our parents and grandparents did it. In traditional societies, the social, economic and political aspects of life are connected. One's share in distribution is tied to one's social status, as well as one's family or kinship relations. The leader gets the best, but no one is allowed to starve.

Tradition is a powerful force even in complex societies. As Western-European societies evolved, particularly with the advent of the Industrial Revolution, the role religion played in shaping economic life changed dramatically. In fact, sociologist Max Weber argues that the Protestant Reformation was critical to the advent of industrialism in England, i.e. the Protestant work ethic spawned a "salvation through hard work and accumulation" mentality which was crucial to the success of early capitalists.

The very longevity of some programs, policies, and practices in church or economic life suggests that they are meeting basic needs and should not necessarily be discarded. But tradition can also be maintained purely by entrenched power, by prejudicial attitudes, or by lack of imagination and creativity.

The role of women in our modern economies is still limited by tradition, buttressed by the prejudice called sexism. Although gains have been made in recent years, the overall pattern remains clear. Men control the vast majority of positions of wealth, power and influence in our political and economic life. Jobs traditionally done by women have lower salaries. When women work in jobs traditionally dominated by men, they earn significantly less.

While various arguments have been put forth to explain or defend this situation, the role that tradition-fueled sexism plays in our economy is not hard to see. The practice of sexism is ethically repugnant from a Christian perspective and fails to make full economic use of an important resource.

What are the strengths and weaknesses of using "tradition" in making economic decisions?

SOME EXAMPLES

Can you think of some different types of economies you have read about or experienced? Here are some examples:

Feudal—a class system generally agriculturally based, with lords who own the land and serfs or peasants who work it.

Barter—people exchange goods or services directly, rather than using money as a medium of exchange.

Slave—one class dominates another by denying people's freedom and ability to own productive resources; historically, this is often based on racial/ethnic differences.

Communal—often seen in "traditional" cultures, including those of indigenous peoples in the Pacific and Americas. This involves some sort of family, clan, or extended clan system for producing and distributing goods. In the Western European tradition, communal economies based on religious values include the Shakers, Amish and Mennonites, as well as the Mondragon system of interlocking cooperatives in Spain, started by a Catholic priest.

★

The Command Approach

One way of settling questions of production and distribution in an economy is to allow a group of persons to make those decisions for the rest of us. In command economies, political and economic systems are linked directly.

Highly centralized economies such as China or Cuba demonstrate the command approach. While workers and consumers may have considerable input as the central plan is being developed, ultimately the order comes down from the top. What is to be produced, how and where, who will get it—the plan gives clear answers. Generally, every citizen has a right to share in the distribution because the society is intended to be egalitarian and distribution is needs-based.

While extreme command economies are clearly on the wane, all modern economies have command aspects. Regulation is essential. Laws guarantee private property rights in some instances

but limit those rights in others. Don't try to start a backyard skunk farm in your suburb! There are emission controls for factories and automobiles, minimum wage laws,

safety and health provisions in the work place. The Canadian Health Plan, which polls show to be highly favored by most Canadians, uses a command approach.

Whenever a government, be it democratic or authoritarian, enters the economy in order to exercise its will, it is using *command*. Examples: The Canadian Wheat Board negotiating contracts throughout the world to help the Saskatchewan farmer, or the U.S. Department of Commerce "encouraging"

the Japanese (with implied economic threats), to limit the number of automobiles exported to the USA.

Although no country has been able to maintain its economy purely on the basis of command, economies with a strong command feature have achieved considerable growth in the short run, and have markedly increased the quantity and quality of health care and education delivered to their citizens.

For example, the infant mortality rate in Cuba has been sharply lowered under its command economy. Highly centralized economies can plan unemployment and boom-and-bust cycles out of existence. But there are opportunity costs.

Command economies, while they may be efficient in allocating resources for certain projects, are notoriously inefficient in meeting the rapidly shifting demands of individual consumers. Decisions on what and how much to produce depend on accurate information on everything from people's current needs and wants to available resources and technological advances. Command economies have great difficulty translating this information quickly into production and distribution decisions. They are frequently "out-of-date."

In addition, the limitations on freedom, with the resulting lack of reward for individual initiative or risk-taking, inevitably leads to the search for yet another way of settling questions about production and distribution.

What are the strengths and weaknesses of using the command approach for making economic decisions?

★

The Market Economy

The most powerful force answering questions today of what to produce, how to produce it and where to sell it is "the market."

One can trace the market system to the wandering merchants of the 10th century, and perhaps even further back. Important factors in succeeding centuries were the growth of cities (where tradition loses its grip on society), the Crusades (which had their economic aspects), the growth of nation states, the exploration of the Americas, and the Protestant Reformation (which rejected the long-held Roman Catholic position against loaning money at interest).

In 1776, an English moral philosopher published a book that has had an astonishing impact on subsequent history.

Adam Smith's *The Wealth of Nations* spelled out the theory on which the market system of economics is based. Other thinkers built on his ideas about "the market," which drives nearly every national economy and dominates the global economy in which we live. (Remember, however, that tradition and command have not gone away!)

TRY THIS EXERCISE

You are having a garage sale, and you have made a list of the items you have to sell. Write down the price you are going to ask for the following items:

A bag of golf clubs
An antique salt and pepper shaker
Some 78rpm records
A bicycle
A child's jacket, gently used
A pair of new snow tires
Two cups and saucers from an old set of dishes

How did you determine your prices?

Did you ask yourself, "What is the just price for this item?" Did you try to remember how much you paid for it? Did you say to yourself, "We've gotten so much use out of this, I really should give it away!"

Or did you wonder, "How many people might be interested in this item?" Did you tell yourself, "This a rare item so I can justify a higher asking price." If you frequent such events, you probably tried to remember how much they were asking for similar items at last week's garage sale.

In a market economy, the price is determined not by some inherent worth of the goods but by what someone is willing to pay. Normally, if you think many buyers will be looking for the same object (greater demand, scarcity of supply), the price can be set higher. (At an auction, the rarity of an item will drive up the bidding.)

The simple market of a garage sale demonstrates another aspect of Adam Smith's thought. The theory assumes that buyers use their money in ways that will best satisfy their wants. The market makes no judgment about the different ways people choose to spend their money.

What holds true for goods is equally true of services offered in a market economy: The worth is not an inherent value but what someone is willing to pay. The economic worth of your labor is not necessarily set by the social importance of your work. Otherwise, child care workers would be near-millionaires and luxury car dealers would receive minimum wage.

In a market system, your labor has an economic value based on what someone is willing to pay you for it. We still fight against that notion. We may look at a piece of modern art and mutter, "Somebody paid a million dollars for that?!" Or we may be amazed to read the dollar amounts in the latest contract signed by a professional football or ice hockey star. In our psyches we think there ought to be a just wage and a just price. The market system says, "No. What is fair depends on supply and demand."

★

Obviously the national and global economies dominated by the market approach are more complicated than our garage sale. More factors are involved than the laws of supply and demand.

Adam Smith and his followers believed that if all people pursue their own interests—that is, cast their dollar votes—then magically (his phrase was "by an invisible hand"), the system will operate for the benefit of all. However, it doesn't take high powers of observation to note that things haven't worked out that way.

The market system assumes that everyone is able to participate in markets—that is, that everyone has something that others are willing and able to buy. Stated another way, one's share in the distribution of goods and services depends on one's ability to earn a decent income—that is, to sell one's labor at a price that will buy what one needs or wants.

"THERE'S A RUMOR GOING AROUND THAT MONEY ACTUALLY EXISTS. BUT UNTIL I SEE SOLID PROOF, I'M SKEPTICAL."

TRY ANOTHER EXERCISE

Mr. and Mrs. Johnson have rented a cottage for a month. They agree that they want to have plenty of free time together, but they also want to prepare a substantial evening meal and straighten up the cottage six days a week.

Mrs. Johnson does both of these jobs more quickly than her husband. She can prepare in one hour a meal which requires two hours of Mr. Johnson's time, and she can clean up the cottage in one hour and fifteen minutes, compared to his one and a half hours.

If their goal is to accomplish both jobs in the least amount of time, how should they divide up the work? Try various arrangements.

If it's okay, I'll come to dinner when Mrs. J cooks.

Economists would say Mrs. Johnson has an *absolute advantage* over Mr. Johnson in both jobs, but a *comparative advantage* in preparing the meal. That is, the time saved is even greater there. For both tasks to get done with the least total amount of time spent, it would be better for Mrs. Johnson to cook all the meals and Mr. Johnson to do all the cleaning. The total time saved would be greater, they would accomplish their goal of more free time together, and both would work less than if they had taken turns cooking and cleaning.

Doing the mathematics shows that if they share the jobs equally (each does half of each job), the total time required is more than 17 hours. If they specialize and use their comparative advantages, the jobs are done in 15 hours.

This concept may seem fairly obvious, but it was not clearly developed until David Ricardo stated it about 150 years ago.

Market economists argue that nations as well as individuals are better off if they use their comparative advantages. Country A may have a comparative advantage in assembling electrical appliances because of low labor costs; country B, with a highly educated labor force, may have a comparative advantage in technological research. In theory, say the market advocates, both countries will gain if they concentrate on their own areas of comparative advantage and trade with the other countries.

As we shall see later, the real world does not always work that precisely or nicely!

Specialization brings problems, too. In our example, the Johnsons might find it more fun to work together on both jobs, or less monotonous to take turns cooking and cleaning. Either tactic might stimulate them to work better. As individuals and nations move toward specialization and using their comparative advantages, we will see significant changes in employment practices and business decisions. Some will benefit; others will be hurt.

A central aspect of a market system is the priority it gives to *efficiency*. Consider this illustration.

My wife and I are washing the windows of our house. Now, assuming that the quality of our window-washing is the same, is it better for each of us to work separately for one hour on different windows, or for us to work together for one hour on the same windows?

In both cases, two hours of labor will have been expended, but any window washer knows that more windows will be cleaned if we have worked together. We will have been more *efficient* in the use of our labor.

We could get into quite a discussion here of the relative merits of cooperation vs. competition. Does competition always spur a better product? Or do partnership and collaboration sometimes produce higher quality efforts?

Economists talk about labor and other resources used in production as *input*, and the results of production as *output*. If you are efficient, you squeeze as much output as possible from the various inputs. In a market system, the purpose of efficiency is to minimize costs, thus maximizing profit, in the belief that all will benefit in the process.

Two observations must be made. In a global economy, it is essential to make the best use of scarce resources. But this efficiency does not assure fair distribution of goods and services, and one of our concerns as Christians is justice for all.

It is equally clear that there is little chance of improved distribution without efficiency in production. So, we should say that *efficiency* is a necessary but not sufficient basis for economic justice. That is true whether we are concerned about health care delivery or affordable houses or pollution-free automobiles.

Another factor present in all types of economic systems but most obvious in the market system where changes are made frequently and rapidly is the cost of making a transition.

When we changed from horse-and-buggy transportation to the automobile, costs were involved. New materials had to be purchased or developed, factories had to be built, assembly lines designed. But in addition to start-up costs, one has to factor in the jobs, even businesses, that have been lost. While eventually more jobs and businesses were created by the development of a new mode of transportation, in the short term, someone had to pay a price for the transition.

Economists look at the *transition costs* of any change in production or distribution. An example on a massive scale can be seen in Eastern Europe as new nations struggle to shift from a *command* to a *market* economy. Thousands have lost their jobs, but by the end of the decade, many thousands of new jobs may have been created.

Free trade can bring about the same dislocation. Whatever we believe about how many will benefit in the long run, it's clear that in the short term, some jobs will be lost and some businesses destroyed.

Imagine yourself in such a situation. If you had lost your job and had no money to meet mortgage payments, would you be comforted with the announcement that, "In the long run, things will be better?" Will you have confidence that things will be better for you? One economist wrote: "In the long run, we are all dead!"

Obvious as the concept of transition costs may be, it was not developed clearly until the 1930s. In fact, the 1991 Nobel Prize in Economics was awarded to retired professor Ronald Coase in part for the way he spelled out the importance of *transition costs*.

Their significance for personal and public economic planning cannot be overemphasized. If no one spells out the *transition costs*, who is going to pay them, and what assistance is available to the "losers," then one can expect resistance to change no matter how valuable it might be for the public good.

Why does the United States Congress repeatedly approve military expenditures which the Pentagon says it does not want? Because jobs would be lost in specific congressional districts and there are no provisions to care for those who would have to pay the short-term *transition costs*.

What are the *transition costs* of building a massive new power generating system in northern Quebec and who will pay them?

What are the strengths and weaknesses of the market approach in making economic decisions?

In today's global economy, all national economies are driven by tradition, command, and market forces. While the market is the predominant approach, useful economic policies do not emerge from arguing about whether socialism or capitalism is the best economic arrangement. Nor about whether a market economy is preferable to a command system.

The relevant question is what is the best mix of tradition, command, and market in each sector of the economy.

What is the best mix:

For delivering mail, as opposed to health care?

For assuring equal opportunities in the job market for racial/ethnic minorities and women?

For controlling earth-destroying pollution?

For producing and distributing food, clothing or any of the hundreds of other items we use every day?

For providing the infrastructure (roads, bridges, buildings, communication and transportation systems), on which any modern economy depends?

For offering quality education to all persons?

For retraining persons whose jobs were eliminated in the search for greater efficiency, or because an old market was replaced by a new?

For eliminating the poverty and hunger which two-thirds of the world's people endure?

What do we want our economic systems to do? List at least three goals for either Canada or the United States, or think globally and list some worldwide guidelines.

1.

2.

3.

★

In writing your goals, did you think about aspects of the Christian faith discussed in Part 2? For Christians, the gospel will provide important criteria, but in fact most people in the world probably would list similar goals:

■ **Fair distribution of income**
Most people would agree that a permanent underclass of people living in poverty in their nation or the world is unjust and unnecessary. But how do we define a "fair" distribution of income? Controversy swirls around not only to what degree, if any, income disparities are acceptable, but also how to close the gap.

■ **Full employment**
While some may argue over the technical meaning of the term, few would dispute that the goal of an economy should be to provide jobs for all who want and are able to work. Defining what we mean by "work" is important. When I have the privilege of caring for a couple of preschool-age grandchildren, it is enjoyable, but daily child care is work! Important issues are related to employment, such as a decent wage, safe working conditions, and involvement in decision-making.

■ Restoring and retaining the health of the planet
If my lumbering job is at stake, I may argue against preserving a particular patch of old forest. But scientific evidence increasingly points to the fact that the way we produce and consume is literally suicidal. Yet, many people believe that we cannot have an acceptable standard of living if we do not have a "growing" economy. Others point to the need for a massive simplification of Northern lifestyles as critical to this aim. Poor people in the North question where this leaves them. Poor people in the South question where the Northerners' environmental worries leaves them as well.

RAESIDE
TIMES-COLONIST
V'ctoria, B.C.
ANADA

■ Developing a peacetime economy
Most citizens of Canada and the United States believe that we need some kind of military defense capacity. But few would believe that our economies require major military expenditures in order to operate successfully. Nevertheless, many citizens will press their government representatives to save a weapons plant or military installation that means jobs in their communities. Powerful corporate interests, supported by workers whose jobs are at stake, will continue to lobby for new,

possibly unnecessary but certainly profitable weapon systems. Particularly in the United States, the shift away from an economy with a major military component will have sizable *transition costs*.

■ Freedom

People prefer freedom, in all aspects of life. Christians, however, will want to keep individual freedom in tension with the good of the community. We will differ sharply over specific applications to economic freedom, but we will all stand somewhere between no freedom at all to make our economic decisions and an absolute right to do anything we want with our economic resources.

■ Equity and diversity

Our economies have privilege embedded into them—privileges for certain classes, castes and ethnic groups, for men over women, and sometimes for certain age groups over others. Many see eliminating sexism, racism, ethnic rivalries, nationalism, etc. as critical to bringing about a more equitable economy at home and in the world. They seek not some grand cultural homogenization, but a system that respects and enables cultural integrity for different peoples.

■ Stability

We read with dismay of economies in which the inflation rate is over 1000 percent. Prices change daily. Money is virtually useless. We prefer a system in which the hills and the valleys are not too steep nor frequent. The current crisis in health care in the United States is caused partly by the lack of stable prices in that area. Without stability, persons on fixed incomes inevitably suffer. In a modern economy, prices across the board do not drop unless there is a major recession. Boom-and-bust cycles may be inevitable in a market economy, but nevertheless stability is a goal sought by all.

■ Growth

Here we begin to run into more divergent opinions. Some insist that growth inevitably harms the environment. Others claim that the industrialized nations' greediness for growth has doomed the rest of the world to continuing misery. Some people in developing nations claim that talk about limiting growth worldwide is yet another attempt to "keep them in their place." Studies show that the vast majority of people in the U.S. and Canada want economic growth in terms of greater purchasing power. But everyone also would like to see their economy produce growth in health care, education and services to those in need.

• Efficiency

This goal is not likely to show up on most opinion polls. But most economists insist that unless resources are used efficiently, to produce maximum results, none of the other goals can be achieved.

You may have used different words, but most of our goals are probably the same. Now comes the difficult part.

It is probably not possible to achieve all of these goals fully nor even to make progress toward them all simultaneously. Concern for the environment or moving to a peacetime economy may result in temporary unemployment, or permanent underemployment, for workers. Achieving full employment might make prices less stable. So choices must be made. Priorities must be set.

Again, the Christian faith will be our chief basis for prioritizing, but some economic knowledge will be required if our priorities are to be translated into viable programs.

Economic Relationships

People have been making economic transactions across community and national boundaries for a very long time. In his brief history of economics, Robert Heilbroner writes:

> Communities have traded with one another at least as far back as the last Ice Age. We have evidence that the mammoth hunters of the Russian steppes obtained Mediterranean shells in trade, as did also the Cro-Magnon hunters of the central valleys of France. In fact, on the moors of Pomerania in northeastern Germany, archeologists have come across an oaken box, replete with the remains of its original leather shoulder strap, in which were a dagger, a sickle head, and a needle—all of Bronze Age manufacture. According to the conjecture of experts, this was very likely the sample kit of a protoype of a travelling salesman, an itinerant representative who collected orders for the specialized production of his community.
>
> (*The Making of Economic Society*, Robert Heilbroner, [Englewood Cliffs, NJ:Prentice-Hall, Inc., 1980], 23)

The major players in today's global economy increasingly perform as if national boundaries do not exist. Of course they do exist, as do the rules and regulations that go along with them, and the struggles to create the European Community or the North American Free Trade Zone show how powerful national interests continue to be. But the trend is clear. "In the global economy, 'trickle down' has been replaced with 'trickle out,' " writes economist Robert Reich. "[Savers] race to wherever around the globe they can get the highest returns." (*The New York Times*, 3 November 1991)

Manufacturers will establish plants wherever they find a labor market and other conditions that will increase their efficiency and therefore their profits. Stock markets are increasingly tied together, around the world and around the clock. It is quite likely that West Coast provinces and states may link their economic hopes more closely to the Asian nations of "the Pacific Rim" than to the rest of Canada and the USA.

The car I drive was designed by Japanese engineers, made of parts manufactured in half a dozen different countries, assembled in a largely automated factory in Mexico, shipped in trucks owned and operated by U.S. citizens and sold as an "American car."

A member of my congregation is the Japanese executive vice-president of a firm that employs 45 Japanese engineers and 600 Americans. The plant makes fuel injection systems for a factory that assembles Honda automobiles in Ohio and markets them as "Japanese cars."

Major Canadian corporations such as Varity, Hiram Walker, Crush International and Stelco make an increasing share of their profits from investments and sales in Latin America. It is now widely accepted that by the end of this century, the world will have three multinational economic blocs: the Pacific Rim nations of Asia, the three countries of North America, and the European Community.

The cause of this globalization of the economy is primarily technological. Alvin Toffler, whose 1970 book *Future Shock* described the rapid changes that confront us all, believes that nations should properly be described as either "fast" or "slow." The increased speed of transportation and the virtually instantaneous transmission of information may make previous economic arrangements obsolete. He points to the bar code on a box of cereal, the scanner at the supermarket, and the creation of computers that will transmit three billion bits of information per second as the forerunners of a radically new 21st century economy.

This acceleration already has produced startling changes. Only a decade ago, some apparel companies moved their manufacturing operations to Third World countries to take advantage of low labor costs. Now, they realize that rapid modes of transportation will allow them to maintain lower inventories and change styles more quickly. Labor costs are no longer the primary factor in their economic decision-making, and some manufacturing is moving back to the

Dee Dee's NEW JOB...

industrialized world. Haggar Apparel, a Texas-based corporation, now stocks its 2,500 customer stores with slacks every three days instead of the seven weeks it once required.

The competitive game in this global economy is no longer limited to so-called developed countries—Canada, USA, Japan, and Europe. A group called the Newly Industrialized Countries (NICs) has joined the ranks of the top 20 exporting nations. The largest plastic manufacturer in the world is in Taiwan; the largest petrochemical firm is in Saudi Arabia; the largest selling import car in Canada in 1990 was the Pony, made by the Hyundai Corporation in the Republic of South Korea. The economic growth rate in most of these countries is well above that of Canada or the United States.

These countries are not only competitors on the world scene; increasingly, they represent new markets. The California Department of Commerce estimates that the nations of the Pacific Rim represent a market that is growing at the rate of $3 billion (U.S.) per week!

India, Thailand and Indonesia are already replacing Taiwan and South Korea in certain industries. The number of players continues to grow. Nevertheless, our present global economy continues to keep most of the world's population in misery.

As we move inexorably to a global economy, five interrelated factors continually surface:

1. Trade arrangements
2. Third World debt
3. Development practices in Third World countries
4. Foreign aid which the industrialized world provides
5. Transnational enterprises/multinational corporations

We will have a chance to look at them more closely in Part 4.

KAL
BALTIMORE SUN
Baltimore
USA

In A Global Economy, Who Wins?

More players in this game, but most of the world still lives in misery.

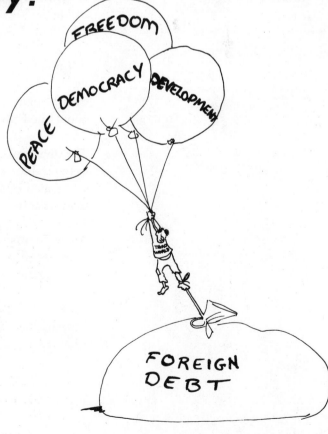

Freer Trade or More Protectionism?

Freer trade refers to any policy or practice which removes barriers to the free movement of goods or services between countries. Protectionism is just the opposite, the erection of barriers to the free movement of goods and services.

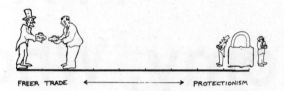

FREER TRADE ←————————→ PROTECTIONISM

Where do you come down in the debate between the two ends of the continuum? More importantly, why is that your position? Even more importantly, what role does your Christian faith play as you consider this question? Before you read on, place yourself on the continuum above. Can you identify with any of the situations described at right?

A wheat farmer in Manitoba who, because of the Canada-U.S. Free Trade Agreement, no longer receives a transportation subsidy if he ships to the USA by western ports.

A North American family convinced that their government's protectionist trade practices cost them more than $1,500 per year.

A Canadian textile worker, one of an estimated 315,000 persons who lost their jobs in the first three years of the Free Trade Agreement.

A Mexican peasant woman who is employed in a U.S.-owned plant just inside the Mexican border for $4.80 a day—four times as much as she has ever earned before.

A Texas family, living below the poverty level even though the father works 40 hours per week at minimum wage. They've just been informed that the plant will close and move to Mexico, where the minimum wage is about one-fifth as much.

The owner of a small manufacturing firm in Illinois who is committed to the welfare of his employes but finds he cannot compete in a market dominated by large firms whose labor costs overseas are drastically lower than what he must pay.

An economist whose studies satisfy him that free trade will benefit everyone in the long run, but who recognizes that there are no structures in place to protect those who will be hurt if free trade is implemented.

Keeping that "family" of persons in mind, put down your ideas about what trading arrangements would be efficient and just.

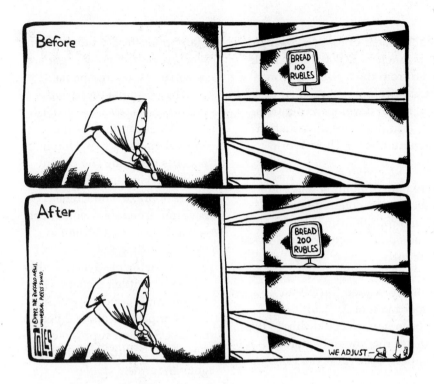

The argument for freer trade

Almost any economist would agree that in a perfect world with each democratically governed country using its comparative advantage to do what it does best, free trade would benefit everyone. We do not live in a perfect world, however. In the real world, what are the advantages of removing restrictions from the free flow of goods and services among nations?

Free traders believe that the market can determine production and distribution patterns for the whole world as well as for one country. Some would add that freer trade also promotes an interdependence among nations that contributes to the search for peace. Freer trade forces companies to be more efficient, to modernize and to meet the highest standards

being set anywhere in the world. For example, Japanese auto makers met strict emission standards 20 years ago while American automakers, partially protected from a free world market by their government, are still dragging their feet. (It should be noted that the Japanese firms raised their standards under pressure from their government rather than from the market.)

Free traders recognize that some workers will suffer short-term job losses as their country moves to a freer trade system, but believe retraining and relocation help can offset this loss. Ultimately, they say, even more jobs will be created. Free traders acknowledge that the benefits gained in some countries will not be fairly distrib-

uted among the people, but believe this issue should be dealt with through internal political change.

In making their case, free traders point to what happens when nations try to protect their industries with quotas, tariffs, regulations and subsidies.

How can Canadian farmers, who depend on export sales, compete with Europeans whose products are being subsidized at far higher rates? American rice growers receive a subsidy one-tenth that of growers in Japan. Protectionist policies invite retaliation from other countries. Free traders say tariffs approved by the U.S. Congress in 1930 deepened the Great Depression.

Placing limitations on free trade inevitably raises prices. An average family's living costs may be increased by as much as $2,000 due to trade limitations. Peanut butter has been removed from the U.S. school lunch program because of its protectionist-inflated price.

Nor are the problems limited to those between developed countries. James Bovard, author of *The Fair Trade Fraud*, summarizes the situation that existed between the United States and a number of Third World countries in 1991:

"The United States will dole out more than $16 billion in foreign aid this year. Yet, while American politicians are congratulating themselves on their generosity, American protectionism is devastating dozens of third-world countries. Our trade policy seems custom-made to keep the third-world barefoot and pregnant, forever reliant on US handouts.

"The US import quota on sugar has bushwhacked Caribbean farmers. Between 1981 and 1988, the Department of Agriculture slashed the amount of sugar that Caribbean nations could ship to the US by 74%. The State Department estimates that the reduction in sugar import quotas cost third-world nations $800 million a year.

GOMAA
AL ALAM AL YOUM
Cairo
EGYPT

Many poor third-world farmers who previously grew sugar are now harvesting marijuana.

"The US quota on peanut imports is so strict that it allows each American to have the equivalent of only two foreign peanuts per year. The peanut quota hurts peanut farmers in Senegal, Brazil, and China. The beef import quota—which costs consumers almost $1 billion a year, according to the Agriculture Department—has throttled Argentine cattle ranchers. The cotton import quota—which limits imports to about 2 percent of the US cotton supply—chokes Egyptian, Pakistani, and Paraguayan farmers.

"The US imposes surtaxes on imports when government officials believe that foreign producers received a government subsidy. The US imposed a 1 percent surtax on Thai rice imports in 1986—even though the US government was giving American farmers a hundred times more in subsidies than the Thai farmers were receiving. The US imposed a surtax on Argentine wool in 1983, even though the Agriculture Department was giving American wool growers 25 times more in subsidies. . .

"Similarly, many third-world nations have been hurt by the US steel import quotas. In 1985, the US forced Venezuela and Mexico to reduce their steel exports to the US by 62%. Trinidad and Tobago have also been adversely affected." (*Christian Science Monitor*, 21 October, 1991)

We must ask ourselves, "Why does the U.S. government impose these quotas?" Is the government protecting small farmers? Or infant industries? Or are powerful lobbies the chief explanation of these practices?

While free traders often argue their case in terms of the negative effects of protectionism, the position is rooted in the conviction that the economy benefits from as little governmental "interference" as possible. Left pretty much to itself, they say the market will get the job done.

Of course, "getting the job done" may take some time, during which job-losers have to fend for themselves. In good times, jobs may be available. In a recession or depression, those who have lost jobs may not be able to find others, in which case they will need government assistance.

The case for some kinds of protectionism

Imagine that you are a citizen of an island nation called Potemkin. You want to start a small business, manufacturing tropical sport shirts. As you begin, your production costs per shirt are considerably higher than those of similar imported shirts from Hong Kong and South Korea. Wouldn't you like some protection from this competition until you can improve your efficiency? In fact, wouldn't you feel entitled to such protection from your government, because you're a citizen and "they" are foreigners? Of course!

Virtually every economist would accept this as a valid form of protectionism. They call it the "infant industry" exception. The problem is determining when the infant has grown up. Such industries understandably will want to keep their privileged position as long as possible.

Most people also will agree that ethical and political considerations will affect the trade arrangements with certain nations at given times. No nation will knowingly permit trade with its enemy in a time of war. Economic sanctions against South Africa in the 1980s were widely practiced.

Unfortunately, governments are seldom consistent in their application of ethical standards. Political and economical considerations seem to outweigh moral positions. In 1991, the United States still had a strict trade embargo against Vietnam, claiming various human rights abuses. But China, while clearly violating human rights, was given "most favored nation" status.

What about a nation's right to protect its culture? The Canadian government insists that radio stations there must include a substantial amount of Canadian-created material. Is this good or bad? Should we rejoice that Coca-Cola and McDonald's are to be found in every corner of the globe?

We may believe that people have a right to preserve their cultures, and we may believe that a multicultural world is a more interesting place in which to live—but then we will have to help those cultures avoid domination by stronger, wealthier nations, or transnational enterprises.

Those who support some kind of protectionism worry about the job losses that occur as nations move toward freer trade. During the first three years of the Canada-U.S. Free Trade Agreement (FTA), which was signed early in 1989, some 315,000 jobs were lost, according to the Ecumenical Coalition for Economic Justice, a Canadian church consortium. Highest job losses were experienced by women and immigrants.

New jobs are being created, but at lower wages. When the FTA was proposed, the Canadian government promised that generous adjustment programs would be available for those who lost their jobs. But the government has cleverly avoided such expenditures by refusing to admit that any of the job losses were caused by the FTA. The recession of the early 1990s makes it more difficult to pinpoint the blame.

The North American Free Trade Agreement (NAFTA) formulated in the summer of 1992 continues the debate. The agreement, if approved by the U.S. Congress, will eliminate most barriers to trade among Canada, the United States and Mexico over the next ten years. Similar free-trading blocs are springing up in Central America (Guatemala, Honduras, El Salvador), South America (Argentina, Brazil, Paraguay, Uruguay), Europe (the European Community), Israel and China, and the countries of the former Soviet Union.

Free traders assume that low-skill jobs ought to be moved to low-wage countries and be replaced (in the First World) by high-technology, knowledge-intensive industries. But the Ecumenical Coalition points out that to move Canada in that direction would require extensive government-funded programs in education, technology development and research which are forbidden under the FTA as "unfair" trade practices.

Another danger which some see in the move toward freer trade is a lowering of environmental standards. All free trade agreements talk about a "harmonization" of standards, proposing that nations adopt the same environmental practices. Furthermore, no nation would be allowed to have higher standards than those set in the trade agreement.

Supporters of freer trade see harmonization as a way of improving the environmental safeguards in many Third World countries but critics are convinced that the standard will be the lowest common denominator. Canada, for example, which has licensed 20 percent fewer active pesticide ingredients and seven times fewer pesticide products than the United States, will be under great pressure to lower its standards as a result of the Free Trade Agreement. On the other hand, many Third World nations see pressure for higher environmental standards as yet another example of the industrialized world's interference in their economies.

Another area where free trade agreements seek harmonization is

in the field of patents, copyrights and trademarks. As Robert Weisman argues in the Washington-based *Multinational Monitor* newsletter, "This would enable the multinational food, chemical, and pharmaceutical companies to gather seeds and herbs from the genetically rich Third World, manipulate them with rapidly evolving biotechnical tools, and then patent the new seeds, pharmaceuticals, or other products." (*Sojourners*, June 1991, p. 32)

Argentinian pharmaceutical manufacturers point out another problem that would arise. At present, Argentinian patent laws permit other companies to compete with the patent holder of a drug. The result is that an arthritis drug that currently costs $170 in the United States sells for $35 in Argentina. Current free trade proposals would deny such competition as long as the patent was in force.

This is a particularly important point in light of current efforts to create a free trade zone of Canada, United States and Mexico. Such a massive trading bloc could exert great pressure on other Latin American countries to change their trade policies.

Yet another concern of those who are skeptical about freer trade is that governments would be limited in what they would be allowed to do for the common good of their people.

The free trade argument goes like this. If a firm in Country A has to pay sizable amounts for its share of employee health insurance costs while a firm in Country B has no such costs because of a government-funded health care program, is that not unfair competition? Or if Country A requires firms to spend more on safety measures for its workers than does Country B, then again, competition is unequal. While theoretically the result could be higher safety standards, critics fear that the opposite will occur. Would it be possible to have a government-funded child care program? Or dental care for all? Those questions cannot be answered with certainty, but present and proposed free trade agreements raise doubts.

Critics of freer trade also say:
■ It will drive even more people off the land into the already unmanageable cities.
■ It will make small business owners and farmers in the Third World compete with giant multinational concerns, on unequal terms.
■ By opening up all borders to outside investors, it limits the possibility of a nation controlling its own economic development.

LURIE'S WORLD

GLOBAL CLIMATE TREATY

"May I suggest that we negotiate fast."

Terms of Trade

When economists talk about the "terms of trade," they mean what you can buy for each unit of what you sell. What is the selling price of a bale of hay compared to that of a tractor? How much coffee will buy how much medicine?

While theoretically one might set a "just price" on certain goods or services, or one might charge a price based solely on the cost of labor and materials, in a market economy, the terms of trade are whatever the buyer and seller negotiate. In that theoretical world beloved by the economists, trade benefits everyone. Obviously a buyer will not purchase unless the price is "right" (that is, manageable); a seller will only sell at a price she feels is "fair" (that is, advantageous). The supply of a product and the demand for it will determine the price and therefore the terms of trade.

There is some truth in that theory. If coffee production increases worldwide, while the demand stays the same (after all, you can only drink so many cups a day), then the price of coffee will drop. When soft drink manufacturers substituted artificial sweeteners for sugar in their products, thus reducing the demand for sugar, the price of sugar dropped.

However, if a group of sellers controls a large share of the supply for a given product much wanted by the buyers, then the sellers can set the price. If they don't have to negotiate, the market does not operate freely.

Oil is an obvious example. The Organization of Petroleum Exporting Countries (OPEC) cartel is able, more or less, to set the price of oil because it controls much of the supply and the world's demand for oil stays high. However, if the 1991 breakthrough in controlled nuclear fusion eventually produces safe, cheap energy, then the price of oil will drop. A cartel of banana growing countries would be less successful at controlling the price since buyers could easily change their eating habits. While price-fixing is illegal in most national economies, it cannot yet be prevented in the global economy.

Cartels are not the only barriers to the free operation of the laws of supply and demand. As we have already discussed, protectionist measures skew prices. But in addition, suppose a child you love is very ill, and you learn that only a certain drug will cure him. How much are you willing to pay or trade for that medicine? If you are desperate enough, you will pay whatever the seller demands. The sale of illegal drugs also illustrates the principle.

What are some other factors in determining the price people pay for things?

However the terms of trade have been determined in the world today, it is clear that they are working to the detriment of the developing countries. A tractor that could be purchased with 10 bales of Sri Lankan tea in 1960 now costs far more than that. The prices of raw products, on which Third World countries depend for export earnings (70 percent for most developing countries; 90 percent for oil-producing nations), are very unstable.

Despite efforts of the United Nations through its Trade and Development Agreements, such changes have brought havoc to some countries. When the International Tin Agreement collapsed in 1986, Bolivia found its economy in shambles. The less-developed countries have proposed that the prices of commodity goods (raw products), and manufactured goods be linked so that they rise and fall together. Free marketeers, of course, vigorously object to such interference in the market mechanism.

Third World Debt

"Being in debt" has a negative connotation in individual or family life. But some debts may be beneficial. People go into debt to buy an automobile. Virtually no one could buy a house without a mortgage. The majority of small businesses begin with borrowed capital. How many students are able to complete graduate school without amassing sizable debts? Debts serve a useful economic function when the borrowed money is used to enhance our capacity to increase our income, and therefore our ability to repay the debt.

Countries also can borrow money for useful purposes—to build roads or train personnel or construct factories or purchase seed and fertilizer, all of which enable goods and services to be produced and sold, so the loan can be repaid.

Of course, both individuals and countries can go too deeply into debt or use the borrowed monies in ways that simply deepen their problems. But even these circumstances do not always create a crisis. In 1984, the United States became the world's #1 debtor nation; it has continued to amass ever greater deficits each year since. Debt has had a major economic and political impact in the USA, but politicians and economists have not treated it as a crisis. (Note that the much-discussed and sometimes-deplored foreign investment in the USA is a major factor in keeping the debt from reaching a crisis state.)

Why, then, do we refer to the Third World debt as a crisis?

Let's begin with a quiz.

THIRD WORLD DEBT QUIZ

1. Third World debt refers to money that less developed countries owe to the United Nations.
   True_____; False_____.

2. Private banks first made large loans to developing countries to help out the economies of those countries.
   True_____; False_____.

3. Most developing countries used almost all borrowed monies for economic or educational projects.
   True_____; False_____.

4. In this century, the United States has never been in debt to other countries or to foreign banks.
   True_____; False_____.

5. The real crisis of debt for developing countries began with the first increase of oil prices.
   True_____; False_____.

6. Developing countries cannot pay off their debt because they cannot export enough raw materials.
   True_____; False_____.

7. The interest rate on past loans to developing countries fluctuates with the interest rates in the industrialized world.
   True_____; False_____.

8. The International Monetary Fund pays the loans of countries that are unable to make loan payments.
   True_____; False_____.

9. Most developing countries probably could pay off their loans if they would change to market capitalism.
   True_____; False_____.

10. The original amount of money loaned to Third World countries has been repaid in the form of interest.
    True_____; False_____.

11. Some debts have been forgiven.
    True_____; False_____.

★

As you read on, you should be able to self-score this quiz. You may decide that some questions must be answered "partly" true or false. The economic and political situations in every country are subject to rapid change, so examples for today may be out-of-date tomorrow.

Since economic issues are very real human problems, let's look at another group of persons in our global family, this time persons who are caught up in the Third World debt crisis:

A mother and father raising their four children on her salary of $75 a month—or $75 a year!

An active church leader who is a director of the Canadian Imperial Bank of Commerce in Toronto.

A small-scale farmer in Brazil whose land has just been expropriated to grow more coffee for export.

A senior staff member of the International Monetary Fund with a deep concern for improving the conditions under which most of the world's poor must live.

A Kansas farmer who must export wheat or lose his farm.

The Minister of Economic Affairs of a Third World country.

A Canadian worker whose employment depends on her company's continuing ability to sell products overseas.

A wealthy businessman in the Third World.

A middle-class taxpayer in the United States or Canada.

A retiree who depends on the interest from bank deposits for some of her income.

That is quite a list, but as we shall see, each is affected by what has happened in the countries where two-thirds of the world's people live.

Looks like oil money greased alot of palms.

The source of the problem

Many explanations of the Third World debt crisis begin with the quadrupling of oil prices in 1973. But since World War II, the industrialized nations have pushed a model of export-oriented growth for the Third World. Developing nations would export raw materials and simple products, while the industrialized world would export manufactured goods.

The theory of comparative advantage provided the rationale. But in the real world, a problem was inevitable. Developing nations can't make enough from their low-priced items to purchase the high-priced manufactured goods offered by the industrialized nations. Even worse, countries that once were food-sufficient no longer are.

The problem escalated when OPEC placed vast dollar earnings in the banks of the industrialized world. Banking representatives claim that what happened next was a standard economic decision, even a generous one: Third World countries needed funds and the banks needed to invest their new income. Critics read the decision otherwise.

To realize what went on, think about going to your friendly local bank for a loan. In addition to providing information about the purpose of the loan, you must demonstrate your ability to repay it, with interest. Your credit rating will be evaluated.

(A football player in the USA who had just signed a multi-year,

★

$12 million contract was refused a credit card until his father would co-sign the application. He had never borrowed money, so he had no credit rating!)

If you were hoping to buy a house, which would involve a large loan and therefore a long repayment period, you probably would be offered a choice between a mortgage with a fixed rate of interest or one with an adjustable rate, which would change (within limits) as national rates fluctuated.

But in offering very large sums to Third World countries, the banks followed none of these procedures. As one young loan officer put it, they were in the business of "selling money." The banks paid little attention to how the loan monies would be spent.

While "country-risk analyses" were prepared to show repayment possibilities, these were based on statistics given by the borrowing

a great time to lay foundations [in Mexico] for 1983 and beyond." (*Selling Money,* S.C. Gwynne, [Wiedenfeld and Nicolson, New York, 1980], 70)

In August 1982, Mexico announced that it was unable to repay its largely commercial loans. Subsequently, countries throughout Latin America and Africa faced the same situation. By 1987, the banks had recognized that many of these loans would never be repaid—but they continued the myth of financial stability by rolling over loans that should have been radically refinanced or cancelled outright.

countries. The banks knew the information was suspect. In one case, the country's population projections were shown to be 60 percent off, and capital available for development was overestimated by tens of billions of dollars. The banks offered loans on a short-term basis only, which meant they could renegotiate to their own advantage as interest rates rose.

In 1979, oil prices again increased, more money came to the banks and and more loans followed. When interest rates tripled within a decade, countries had to pay billions in extra debt costs. So new loans were made to allow countries to pay interest on earlier loans. Still the banks continued to pour money in. Only months before certain countries announced that they could not meet their payments, Lloyd's of London reported that the prospect of Brazil overcoming its current difficulties was favorable. A Bank of America officer announced, "We're telling our clients that now is

But what happened to all that money? Some of it was used for much needed development projects and essential public services. But some dictatorial leaders (with whom the banks willingly worked) spent much of it on military hardware, largely to keep their own populations in line. Some went for vast technological projects with little consideration for the countries' economic needs or possibilities.

A very large percentage of the money went from the Third World countries right back to the First World banks, in the form of deposits into the private accounts of corrupt Third World politicians and business elites. Without this "capital flight," Argentina's debt in 1987 would have been $1 billion instead of $50 billion, and Mexico would have owed $12 billion rather than $100 billion. ("International Debt Crisis, Year Five," Walden Bello and Claudio Saunt, *Christianity and Crisis*, 23 November 1987)

As the Roman Catholic Bishops' Conference of Panama summarized the situation: "There has been a squandering and misappropriation of public funds, borrowed from foreign banks."

WHERE DID THE LOAN MONEY GO?

1) FOOD and EDUCATION

2) MILITARY

3) BIG PROJECTS

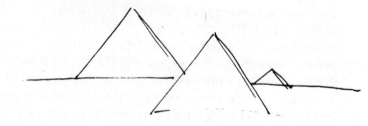

4) CAPITAL FLIGHT

Whatever the motives and practices of the First World's banks, it was clear by the mid-1980s that their loan portfolios were in serious trouble. For help, they turned to the International Monetary Fund. Walter Owensby, of the Presbyterian Church's Social Justice and Peacemaking office in Washington, explains the origins and the changing role of the IMF in his helpful book *Economics for Prophets*:

In 1944, with the end of World War II in sight, leaders of the capitalist industrialized world met in Bretton Woods, New Hampshire, to design the structures of an integrated order designed to prevent a slide back into depression and to facilitate postwar recovery. One of the principal institutions that grew out of those accords was the International Monetary Fund (IMF). Its chief function was to fix and maintain the exchange rates of various national currencies so that countries would not be able to devalue their money in order to make their products cheaper in the world market, thus gaining an advantage in international trade. The IMF also acted as a lender of last resort to countries having a temporary deficit in their balance of payments.

Except for the petroleum crisis and the financial chaos that it caused, the IMF might simply have gone out of business by the mid-1970's. Instead, it embarked upon a new career as overseer, adviser, and disciplinarian of economically troubled nations. There are some 140 countries that are members of the IMF. Representation is not based on the concept of one nation, one vote; it is determined by the amount of money each participant puts in the Fund. Thus the United States holds about 23% of the voting power, the European Economic Community 19%, and the ten richest nations over 50%. The thirty-seven poorest countries control just 6% of the voting power. Not surprisingly, then, the policies of the IMF tend to reflect the perspective and interests of the advanced industrialized nations.

Most Third World nations spend more money on imports than they receive from exports. (This, of course, changes as they fall deeper into debt.) To make up the difference, a country may seek to borrow money from the IMF. The IMF will make such a loan only after a team of IMF experts has conducted an on-site study of the local economy. The goals of the study are simple and straightforward: to ensure that there is enough money to repay the loan when it comes due, and to prevent future balance-of-payment problems. Thus the IMF usually 'recommends' that the country increase net foreign-trade earnings by decreasing imports and increasing exports. The country has little choice but to agree, because the IMF can withhold its seal of approval. This would not only deny the country the IMF loan but also close the doors to commercial credit, since most commercial banks have made their loans to troubled nations contingent upon compliance with IMF recommendations. Without the IMF's seal of approval, a country would likely be denied commercial credit regardless of the need for or the soundness of the specific project for which the loan was sought. As a result, the government is in a weak bargaining position and must essentially comply with whatever measures the IMF might "recommend."

Typically, a country seeking IMF approval must agree to do a number of things: devalue its currency (making its exports cheaper to other countries); reduce the growth in money supply (slowing the economy and cutting consumption); impose wage controls (which help keep costs of production down and make goods more competitive in the international market); reduce government spending (cutting subsidies for food and fuel, social services, and infrastructure investments); promote exports (diverting production away from domestic needs); raise taxes (so that the government will have funds to devote to debt repayment); raise interest rates (to encourage savings and investment); end trade barriers (in order to force national producers to be competitive); and encourage foreign investment.

Needless to say, such economic interventionism is reserved for poor and weak countries; the rich and industrially powerful are presumed wise enough to solve their own problems. Although the U.S. runs huge trade and budget deficits and is the world's largest debtor, the IMF has not attempted to impose its program here.

Walter Owensby, *Economics for Prophets* [Grand Rapids, Michigan: Eerdman's Publishing Co., 1988], 163-164)

"Did you ever try saying 'No' to the U.S. State Department?"

IF YOU POOR NATIONS WANT MORE LOANS, HERE'S WHAT WE WANT TO SEE—

GREATER BALANCE OF TRADE EQUILIBRIUM, APPROPRIATE CURRENCY ADJUSTMENTS...

AND AN END TO SUBSIDIZED CONSUMPTION   WHAT DOES ALL THAT MEAN?

EAT LESS

The Human Costs

While it is possible to describe the problem of Third World debt in economic terms as we have done, it is even more important for us to think of it in human terms. Let's revisit some of the persons we mentioned at the beginning of this section and see the impact of the debt on them.

(If you are reading this book with a group, try taking different roles, and discuss the debt crisis accordingly.)

The poor of the Third World countries:

The IMF-imposed plan caused the price of bread to double and that of kerosene to triple overnight in Bolivia. In Ghana, devaluation of the currency meant that it took one week's wages to buy a loaf of bread. After adjusting for inflation, the annual income of the average Ghanaian has dropped from $600 to $170 since 1980. As incomes have declined and prices increased, women have had to work longer hours both in and out of the home. In most of the Third World since 1980, basic health and educational services available to the poor have been reduced. Primary public school enrollments fell in 103 countries in the 1980s. In many urban areas, the purchasing power of the minimum wage has dropped more than 50 percent in the last decade.

A conscientious banker or IMF officer:

We wish there were a better way and we concede that mistakes have been made. We no longer make loans to regimes with obviously corrupt leadership. We recognize that the denial of human rights is one of the criteria we should use in evaluating loan applications. We accept that the poorest countries should be forgiven much of their past debts provided that they are then willing to take the admittedly difficult steps to become a more market oriented economy. The Structural Adjustment Programs that we insist on, do work. It can be seen in some of the East Asian countries and is now being demonstrated in Tanzania and Chile and Mexico where there has been a steady sustained growth since 1985. There is simply no other alternative which has both economic and political validity.

North American workers/farmers dependent on exports:

Even though industrialized nations mostly trade with other developed countries, the loss of Third World markets can slow down an economy. Further, the devaluation of foreign currencies with the resulting drop in the dollar cost of their exports drives down prices for that product everywhere. The net result is a loss of jobs, a drop in demand for certain products, and lower profits—with a resulting pressure for lower wages.

The elites of Third World countries:

Depending upon their commitment to the welfare of their own people, Third World leaders react to the debt situation in different ways. Some have exploited it for personal gain. In 1986, a Mexico City newspaper published the names of 575 citizens having foreign investments of over one million dollars. (*The New Republic*, 14 April 1986, p. 20) President Mobutu of Zaire is reputed to be one the world's wealthiest persons. But many Third World leaders feel "recolonized," oppressed by economic domination. They are administering their economies in the interests of their creditors, and repaying their debts with the sufferings of their people. As a Jamaican church leader put it: "No reading of scripture would oblige hungry people to starve themselves and their children simply to honour contractual agreements to repay rich people and institutions." ("International Debt Crisis," Task Force on the Churches and Corporate Responsibility, p. 11)

A taxpayer in Canada or the USA:

The taxes we pay involve us in the international debt problem in at least three ways. They provide the funds for our country's foreign aid program and for its contribution to the IMF. Therefore, we have a right and an obligation to evaluate how those funds are being used. Our tax monies also pay the salaries of the public officials who are formulating the nation's policy toward the debt situation. They are our employees and should hear what we as employers think of their work. And in the United States, banks whose failure is largely due to bad loans made at home and abroad are being propped up and bailed out with tax monies.

A retired pensioner:

Part of my income is dependent on the bank's receiving interest on loans made in order that it can pay interest on my deposits. Forgiving loans may be at the cost of reducing my income.

Drugs and the debt

Another seldom discussed aspect of the debt problem is its relationship to the illegal drug trade. A report by the Task Force on the Economic Crisis of the General Board of Global Ministries of the United Methodist Church explains this connection:

Today, drug protection and a sustained economic crisis are two sides of the same coin for many nations. The rapid decline in market prices for traditional exports in the 1980's, mounting foreign debts, chronic poverty, and the steady increase in world market demand for drugs have led to a boom in illicit drug production from Asia to Latin America. As prices for their agricultural products plummeted, tens of thousands of farmers switched to crops such as coca and the opium poppy in order to survive. In many countries, the export of these illicit cash crops has helped boost bank dollar reserves at a time when legal export earnings have dwindled and new loans and investments have dried up.

The Third World Debt crisis has further exacerbated the problem of drug production. Pressured by the international financial community to meet payments on their loans, many drug-producing countries have become increasingly reliant on the dollars generated by the drug trade. Most debtor nations have also been forced to make severe cuts in government spending to appease the creditor bank's watchdog, the International Monetary Fund (IMF). These bitter austerity measures have invariably led to mass lay-offs and wage freezes, forcing many to turn to the most viable economic alternative: the drug economy. . . This has held true particularly for the Andean cocaine-producing countries of Colombia, Peru, and Bolivia, where the links between falling prices for legal exports, the debt crisis, and the growth of the drug trade are clearest." (*Intricate Web: Drugs and the Economic Crisis*, 1990, pp. 40-41)

What can be done about the debt?

It is obvious that the Third World debt problem will have to be solved before much progress can be made toward a just, sustainable global economy. How, though? A number of proposals have been offered:

Write off some of the debt
The United States and Canada have forgiven part of the debts owed to the governments. More could be done in this area. Commercial banks have forgiven portions of uncollectible loans only if payment of the balance was guaranteed by the tax-funded international agencies.

Reduce tariff and quota barriers
The industrialized countries could lower or eliminate tariff and quota barriers for goods produced in developing nations, to enable them to increase earnings. Canada has moved significantly farther than the United States in this area.

Debt-for-nature swap
This is a variety of a debt-equity swap. A foreign creditor (such as a bank) will sell a country's debt at a discount to an international environmental group such as the Nature Conservancy. This group will then use the money to buy a piece of environmentally sensitive property in that debtor's nation to protect it. These deals may be done in consultation with local environmental groups. However, critics say they override traditional land claims of indigenous peoples and give "Northerners" rather than locals the say about how resources are used.

Debt-equity swap
A highly controversial approach to reducing a country's debt. How it works: A foreign bank will sell off a nation's loans at a discount. Multinational corporations buy these loans, and then present them to the central bank of the country for collection. Countries often set up "auctions" where the corporations bid for the right to translate these foreign loans into local currency, to make a local investment. Often this has been used at the same time a country is "privatizing," i.e. selling off public companies to private investors. The end result is that foreign capital may be able to buy up and control a large portion of a country's economy.

Revolving development funds
Some non-governmental groups have proposed that the IMF, World Bank and regional development banks establish a precedent for a kind of revolving development fund which private commercial banks could follow. Instead of forcing a country to pay back loans with foreign currency which the creditor then uses for other purposes, they could allow the debtor to pay back the loan in local currency. Then the government could use that money to invest in local development projects (roads, electrification, sewers, housing).

Different evaluation criteria
A new measure is needed by the World Bank and IMF for evaluating the performance of debtor nations. Existing criteria which emphasize growth, foreign exchange earnings and low inflation, and balanced budgets at all costs. Other objectives need to be factored in. One example is the proposed UN Human Development Index, based on life expectancy, literacy, and purchasing power (per capita annual income). Other proposed measurements focus on environmental protection and public health.

Individualized action
The IMF needs to recognize that not all countries can be treated in the same way. The United Nations Economic Commission for Africa has proposed a new approach that emphasizes more self-sufficiency (especially in food production), the importance of the role that women play in economic development, the need to involve people in designing and implementing small scale projects, and debt repayments that make continuing economic progress possible. Additional loans or grants could be tailored to countries using some of these criteria.

Channel aid differently
Governments could (and sometimes do), channel their foreign aid money through non-governmental organizations (NGOs) and even church agencies because they have good track records of getting the money to the people.

Foreign Aid

Some of the same issues raised by commercial or international agency loans to developing countries again surface as we consider those made either by one nation to another (bilateral aid), or through the World Bank or regional development banks. (The World Bank was created in 1945, at the same time as the International Monetary Fund, to make long-term loans that would assist poorer countries in their development efforts. As with the IMF, the World Bank's decisions are controlled by those countries that have made major contributions to it.)

In considering foreign aid, a Canadian analysis serves well to raise the basic issues.

In 1991, three Canadian ecumenical coalitions published a study of recent aid policies and practices of their government ("What Good Came From It at Last? CIDA: Four Years After Winegard," Inter-Church Fund for International Development and the Churches Committee on International Affairs of the Canadian Council of Churches). They were chiefly responding to an ongoing debate between a tri-party parliamentary committee (Canada has three major political parties), and the executive branch of the government.

In addition to ethical and economic reflections, the churches evaluated how aid programs were being implemented and how they were evaluated by those people whom the programs were intended to help. The churches' overseas partners enabled them to do this.

A 1987 Canadian government report had concluded that past aid programs had been shaped to serve immediate Canadian political and economic goals. Arguing that "the purpose of aid is to aid," however, it said that aid programs

> ## "This diabolical thing you call structural adjustment is not just a bitter pill for us to swallow—it is a poisonous pill that will kill our people."

should help the poorest countries; should emphasize agriculture, primary education, rural health, and the training of the poorest people; should provide additional funds. The government claimed to accept most of these recommendations.

Four years later, church observers concluded that Canada's aid program had failed to follow these guidelines and instead had moved in a different direction. The observers expressed little hope for much immediate change.

The major issue raised by the church report is identical to that raised by the Structural Adjustment Programs of the IMF discussed above. In making loans directly or through the World Bank, the Canadian government insists that all countries adopt the export-driven, free(r) market policies of the industrialized nations. It does so in spite of its own statement that such programs must "take into account their human impact on the people they are designed to help." The government believes that Third World countries are responsible for their poverty because they have failed to take the steps necessary to integrate their economies into the global economy.

The church observers acknowledge that developing countries need to manage their economies differently but it points to the massive suffering that the adjustment programs have caused. That suffering is highlighted in reports sent to the churches from throughout the Third World. A Zimbabwean woman wrote: ". . . it is the poorest who must bear the burdens on their already breaking backs and even their children will not benefit. African people would sacrifice a great deal for the future of their children but this thing— this diabolical thing you call structural adjustment—is not just a bitter pill for us to swallow, it is a poisonous pill that will kill our people."

Aid programs are supposed to help the poorest, but the emphasis on one kind of economic adjustment has widened the gap between the rich and the poor in every country where it has been applied.

The church report also questions the claim that long-term gain will follow short-term pain. It notes that major factors operating in the global economy also contribute to Third World poverty. By insisting that the problems lie only within national economies of the Third World nations, the industrialized nations are able to ignore such factors as their own protective tariffs, the changing terms of trade, the net flow of capital from the South to the North, the lack of Third World-focused research, and the role of multinational corporations.

The over-emphasis on structural adjustment also means that instead of working out its own cooperative arrangements with the countries being helped, Canada increasingly cooperates with the policies of the IMF, World Bank and other industrialized countries. The church report expresses regret that Canada seems to be giving up its role of a non-colonial power that can relate to Third World countries as an equal, and instead is becoming a member of the dominant power group.

The report also notes that in 1970, Canada accepted the internationally recommended goal of putting 0.7 percent of the Gross National Product into aid programs, but it has reduced that percentage steadily and probably will continue to do so.

Like all industrialized countries, Canada usually had required that aid recipients spend a share of the aid money on Canadian goods and services. Although the government theoretically rejected that position

in 1987, the churches report little change. Current aid programs may give aid-receiving countries more freedom in what they will buy, but the purchases are still required.

While all discussion of foreign aid recognizes that human resource development is essential, the question of who will be trained remains unanswered. Shall it be the poorest, to enable them to develop local projects and involve local people in designing and implementing the program? Or shall it be the national economic managers, who can work on changing the structures of the economy? The Canadian government has opted

> **"Perhaps the major lesson . . . is that development will only take place when and where there is effective participation of the people directly affected."**

strongly for the latter group. As one of the churches' Costa Rican contacts put it: "This is not really 'people centered development' or grassroots empowerment. Instead, we're training the bureaucrats of the power structure."

Canada also agreed to consider human rights in making loans, and said it would work to make human rights a criterion for grants made through the IMF and World Bank.

But, says the church report, that promise too seems to have been forgotten. Greater attention has been given to the role of women in development, and to ways of assuring that once begun, the development is sustainable, but human rights have been given very low priority.

The churches conclude their report: "Historically, Canada has often gained its influence and won its reputation by remaining open to alternative strategies that are developed by Third World people and their governments. This openness has proved beneficial, for perhaps the major lesson learned over the past forty years is that development will only take place when and where there is effective participation of the people directly affected, and where their immediate needs are directly addressed."

Fundamental questions about aid between countries are:

■ Does the solution to Third World poverty require every country to adopt the market policies of the industrialized nations?

■ How much of their productive wealth should rich countries give to their poorer world neighbors?

■ How should aid be allocated? What priorities should be followed?

■ Should aid be tied to concern for human rights, democratization, women's place in Third World economies?

■ Should all the developed countries use one aid policy or would greater variety bring more success?

■ Could foreign aid be more helpfully channeled through church and other non-governmental agencies which have a track record of working directly with the people in need?

The Canadian churches addressed these questions in their evaluation of their government's foreign aid program. Think about what you know of U.S. aid policies, and see if the priorities make sense from a Christian perspective. (Note that as of 1990, more than 60 percent of American aid was for military purposes.)

"IT'S...UH... NICE, BUT WHERE DO WE SLEEP?"

Multinational Corporations

Have you ever heard two people describe an event and wondered if they could possibly have been at the same place? That often happens when people talk about multinational corporations or transnational enterprises. If you talk to the chief executive officer of a multinational, he will assure you that his firm is making a significant contribution to all of its stakeholders—employees, owners, customers and the people of the several countries involved. But if you listen to a critic, you will hear multinationals described as purely selfish in intent and satanic in their influence.

These characterizations are not exaggerated. The former head of General Electric stated, "We are stewards for some of the most valuable resources of the nation, or of the world. General Electric is a unique configuration of assets, one of the most productive enterprises on the globe. Those assets are truly significant to the progress of humankind, and must not be squandered, mismanaged, or directed toward socially destructive ends." (*The Corporation, A Theological Inquiry*, Michael Novak and John W. Cooper, eds., American Enterprise Institute, Washington, D.C., p. 140)

In contrast, Dr. Francisco Catao said at a 1981 World Council of Churches consultation: "The churches' action in the world runs directly counter to the action of the TNC's [transnational corporations], which actually oppose justice, favor economic 'disorder' and, in the final instance, constitute the leaven of a society contrary to the spirit of the Good News."

Can we say anything about multinational corporations that will not invite immediate rebuttal?

1. They are here to stay. Corporations which have production branches or subsidiaries in more than one country have been around for a long time, but in the last half-century they have grown in number and size and probably will continue to do so. Global economics cannot possibly be understood without them.

Furthermore, multinational corporations increasingly represent the outreach of "home corporations" that are owned by investors from more than one country and thus should be called "global firms." Some will control every aspect of the production of one particular product—a fast food chain that raises its own beef and chickens in one or more countries, has a fleet of jets and trucks, makes its own packaging, and owns or licenses its own retail stores worldwide. Others will be mergers of corporations with vastly different offerings of goods and services—for example, health foods from one department and banned-from-the-USA/Canada drugs from another.

2. Not all multinationals are the same. Congregational life cannot be judged by someone who has observed only the communities gathered around Jimmy Swaggart or Mother Teresa! It is equally unfair to make an overall judgment about multinational corporations by observing the worst or best practices of some.

3. The reason that firms in the industrialized world have expanded into other countries is, not surprisingly, in order to increase their profits. If Placer Dome Inc. could realize a greater return on its investment by leaving the money in a Canadian bank rather than operating an open pit mine in the Philippines, it would certainly do so. Whether multinational corporations have a special responsibility to consider how they make their profits in other countries is a legitimate question, but in a market economy, we must expect businesses to seek the highest possible return on their investments.

There is increasing evidence that some multinational corporations have engaged in life-destroying activities at home and abroad, around the world. When an Indonesian laborer was electrocuted, a confidential company report admitted that inadequate safety practices were partly to blame. A Colombian doctor testified to his belief that a significant number of deformed babies were related to the pesticides provided by a multinational corporation. When a fire retardant chemical used on children's sleepwear was shown to cause cancer in animals, the garments were ordered off store shelves in the U.S. immediately. However, manufacturers promptly began shipping the garments overseas, defending their action as "not illegal." (Robert Wyrick, *Newsday*, reported in *The Indianapolis Star*, 31 January 1982)

Many supporters of transnational enterprises are distressed by such practices, of course, and would urge the corporations to "clean up their act."

Governments in poorer countries are in a weak position when negotiating with corporations that can provide much needed technology and investment. Many countries do not have the resources or the commitment to determine tolerance levels for dangerous drugs or pesticides. Consumer groups that may provide some check on corporate practices in industrialized countries are usually weak in the Third World and may not be able to contend both with the elites and the governments of their countries. Therefore, it may seem that corporations can do anything they please.

Multinationals: Honor or blame?

Supporters claim that multinational corporations are a sign of a more interdependent world. They bring technology, training, research and management skills to other countries and share with entrepeneurs there. Their plants encourage local industries and businesses to become suppliers, boosting local economies. They provide some taxes for host countries and invest part of their profits there as well. Their research has saved lives through new medical discoveries and increased the food supply with agricultural advances. They have found ways to extract hard-to-reach resources that would otherwise be unused. They have provided jobs, often at wages well above those being paid by indigenous firms. They have forced governments to start building the infrastructure without which development cannot happen. They are the most efficient form of economic cooperation.

But many people, in both the North and South, evaluate multinational corporations very differently. In their single-minded pursuit of profit, such corporations destroy the earth—the rain forest in Brazil, the lakes and rivers of a dozen other countries. They claim to evaluate the risks and benefits of their actions, but actually they risk the welfare of others for the benefit of themselves. They are committed to a model of development that emphasizes industrialization and exports, thus discouraging agricultural self-reliance. They market products regardless of their social worth; tobacco marketing in Asian countries is only one of many examples. When the corporations look for the comparative advantages of poor countries, they see only raw materials and low labor costs, so the structures they create guarantee continuing poverty. By manipulating prices between branches of the company, they pay lower taxes than would otherwise be the case. Their desire for political stability often leads them to

"They claim to evaluate the risks and benefits of their actions, but actually they risk the welfare of others for the benefit of themselves."

deal with corrupt and autocratic government leaders. They have given up national loyalties but have not replaced them with a commitment to internationalism. Instead, a profit-driven paternalism prevails: "Trust us—we'll look after you."

Feelings run high about multinationals. But more helpful than a debate might be a consideration of alternatives that would enhance the advantages and correct the abuses of the present system.

Can the United Nations or some other international agency develop and enforce a code of conduct for multinational corporations? For decades, the U.N. has tried, but the U.S. government has consistently opposed the the effort. Perhaps an international bankruptcy court could be organized, or a forum for international conflict resolution.

As the industrialized world increasingly organizes itself into multi-nation trading blocs, could Third World countries band together to gain greater power in their dealings with the multinational corporations? OPEC shows both the possibilities and the difficulties of such an approach. The price of oil has gone up but the OPEC countries are constantly squabbling over how best to work together.

It does seem that ways must be found to strengthen or reform the major international organizations (such as the IMF, the World Bank and the United Nations), so that developing nations share in the power.

Some economists feel that the rise of transnational enterprises will change our thinking about national economies and the global economy. According to the Secretary of Labor, Robert Reich:

> We are living through a transformation that will rearrange the politics and economics of the coming century. There will be no national products or technologies, no national corporations, no national industries. There will no longer be national economies . . . All that will remain rooted within national borders are the people who comprise a nation. Each nation's primary assets will be its citizens' skills and insights. Each nation's primary political task will be to cope with the centrifugal forces of the global economy which tear at the ties binding citizens together—bestowing ever greater wealth on the most skilled and insightful, while consigning the less skilled to a declining standard of living. (*The Work of Nations*, [New York, A.A. Knopf, 1991] 3)

While Reich illustrates his case from the U.S. economy, his argument applies equally to all national economies. We still believe, Reich contends, that the welfare of all people in a country is somehow related to its "national economy," and that all the citizens go up and down together. We also think that "our" economy competes with the national economies of others. It follows that *our* corporations need to remain strong and that we should be concerned when those others buy our companies or invest too heavily in our economy. These "we-they" assumptions, says Reich, are totally wrong.

The future lies with global firms which have stockholders all over the world and will move money, factories, personnel and technology to gain a higher return on their investment. Therefore, the economic welfare of people in any country will no longer be related primarily to the economic health of that country's corporations but to the job skills the people can offer corporations that may be owned by investors all over the world.

Reich amasses a vast amount of data to illustrate his case: As of 1990, 10 percent of the American work force was employed by foreign-owned firms and the percentage is growing each year. Workers, it turns out, do not care who owns the company if their jobs are satisfactory. On the other hand, 40 percent of IBM employees worldwide are not Americans; less than half of Whirlpool's 44,000 workers live in the USA. General Electric owns a light bulb factory in Hungary. DuPont employs more than 180 Japanese rsearchers at its Yokohama facility. Chrysler intends to build a new corporate supersonic jet with its Soviet partner, using a British-built engine; the plane will be manufactured in eastern Europe. The Japanese hope by 1992 to have 75 percent American-built parts in their cars sold in the USA, a higher percentage than will be in "American" cars. In fact, says, Reich, if you want to "buy American," it would be better to purchase a Honda than a Pontiac Le Mans.

If Reich and like-minded thinkers are generally correct in their analysis of where the world

economy is heading, fundamental economic and political questions face us all. How do Christians understand the role of the nation-state? Should we be concerned if the world is dominated by one homogeneous, essentially material-istic culture? Even if the rich get richer, can a global corporate network also make it possible for the poor of the world to improve their lot? Or will such arrange-ments increase and further institu-tionalize the poverty of the people of the Third World? If Reich is right, the change may be as dra-matic as that created by the Indus-trial Revolution—and the shift in our ways of thinking and living may have to be that dramatic as well.

Multinational corporations are the dominant players in the global economics game. If you are not employed by one of these firms, or if your stock portfolio is negligible, you may think you are not really involved in the issues. But if you own a single share of a mutual fund, or if you are contributing to or receiving money from a pension plan, you probably are a stock-holder in several of the largest multinational firms.

If you are contributing to or receiving money from a pension plan, you probably are a stockholder in several of the largest multinational firms.

Some stock analysts are con-vinced that well before the end of the decade, there will be 1,000 global firms listed on all major stock markets. These firms will constitute a kind of super-blue-chip category, in which pension fund and mutual fund managers will do their chief investing. These international firms will have no allegiance to any one nation (their "owners" will live all over the world), nor to any local commu-nity.

If this scenario proves correct, then many of us will face an ethical dilemma. The security of our pensions will depend upon the economic success of massive corporations that have freed themselves from national or community influence. Will our prime concern be for our present or future economic well-being, or for the welfare of those most affected by these mammoth enterprises—a mother in Africa, a child in Bangladesh or a farmer in the Philippines?

Obviously Somebody needs to get firm with these firms!

5

A Really New Economic Order?

Some new ways to live our faith in an economic world

BADO
LE DROIT
Ottawa
CANADA

READY TO RECYCLE?

So what does all this mean to us? We begin with a question.

How do non-poor Christians in Canada and the United States help themselves and others make decisions which will translate "good news to the poor" into daily realities?

We ask that question as persons who have experienced God's love revealed in the life and teachings, death and resurrection of Jesus Christ.

But why do we limit our question to the non-poor? Because with the rarest of exceptions, those using this workbook are not the poor of North America nor the rest of the world. Most of us will not consider ourselves rich, but we are certainly not poor.

The most important role in bringing in a new order will be played by the poor. The non-poor may have something to contribute to the discussion, and must stand in solidarity with the poor. How? By starting with ourselves, and with our own countries, because that is where our influence is the greatest and where changes need to be made. We must think globally and act locally.

But before we consider what we can be do, we need to deal with some feelings that we may still have.

"I'm still not convinced that this global talk has much to do with me!"

Maybe food feels more relevant than stocks.

North America can produce enough food for its people and for export because of huge increases in per-acre yield over the last 50 years—anywhere from 100 percent for soybeans to 333 percent for corn. Half of this increase is due to the creation of new hybrids, but these hybrids provide a "banquet table" for pests. So farmers shift regularly to different hybrids with new pest resistance.

Scientists find the germplasm for the new hybrids almost exclusively in the forest areas of the Third World. That gives our food supply a global connection. In addition to disease-resistant plants,

research has discovered a wild coffee that has no caffeine and a Paraguayan plant that is 300 times as sweet as sugar, with no calories. Either discovery could have a significant impact in one sector of our economy.

The U.S. Cancer Institute is in a five-year, $8 million program to test native plants in Africa and Latin America for possible cures for cancer and AIDS. Although only 0.2 percent of the known flowering plants have been carefully studied for possible medical use, Dorothy Bray, a pharmacologist, says, "These, directly or indirectly . . . have yielded virtually all the drugs we have on the market today." (*Entangling Alliances*, John Maxwell Hamilton, Seven Locks Press, Washington, D.C., 1990, pp. 82ff)

Global interdependence? You can bet your life on it!

Or, as the minority whip in the U.S. House of Representatives, Newt Gingrich (R-Georgia), puts it: "The world market is real and technology means we really do live on one planet and any kind of attempt to isolate from that is really crazy." (*The Christian Science Monitor*, 21 August 1992, p.4)

"The problem is too big to solve."

We must face this attitude both theologically and practically. To live without hope is to deny the power of God, to live as if the Resurrection had not taken place. The biblical message is "Rejoice in hope" (Rom. 12:12), but we tend to be impatient. We want problems solved totally and immediately, but the kingdom comes "Lo, here; Lo, there." Theologian Paul Tillich wrote, "The kingdom comes here and now in every act of love, in every manifestation of truth, in every moment of joy, in every experience of the holy." (*Christian Century*, 14 November 1990, p. 1066)

And hope can be affirmed by looking about us, not only at what *is*, but at what is *possible*. The major health needs of all the world's children could be met with $25 billion over the next 10 years, about 2.5 percent of what the world currently spends in one year for military expenses. (World Summit for Children, 1990)

Hope is even more visible through daily acts of love and sacrifice throughout the world. Here is an example:

> In Timor in Indonesia during the dry season, children left alone for a few moments while their parents weeded their cassava field found some matches and in a matter of minutes, the beehive-shaped, grass-roofed home was reduced to a pile of ashes. The children fortunately were safe. Seeing that nothing was left of her earthly possessions, the mother wailed. As a small crowd gathered, Petrus, a neighbor, suddenly demanded, "Ayo! Buka pakaian!" He was asking everyone present to take off all the clothes they could and give them to this family. "All of you can go home and put on other clothes," he said, "but this family has nothing. We must help them now." The spirit was catching. Within four days, a new home had been built, dishes and cooking utensils had been loaned and the family had been restored to life. (From a newsletter by John and Karen Campbell-Nelson published in November 1990 by the Stewardship Council of the United Church of Christ.)

Bible scholar Walter Brueggemann has defined hope as "the refusal to accept the reading of reality which is the majority opinion."

"There's really nothing that I can do."

Just finish reading this chapter, and you may change your mind. The Pauline affirmation is valid: "We have gifts that differ according to the grace given to us." (Rom. 12:6)

There is a helpful story from the Jewish tradition. As the saintly Rabbi Zusya lay dying, his close friends gathered around and were surprised to notice that he was crying. "Why do you cry?" they asked. "Because," he said, "when I come before the throne of God, God will not ask me 'Why were you not like Abraham?' because I am not Abraham. And God will not ask me 'Why were you not like Moses?' because I am not Moses." "Then," said his friends, "why are you crying?" "Because God will ask me 'Why were you not Rabbi Zusya?' and I will not know what to answer."

We don't have to do everything, and we don't have to do what everyone else does, but each of us can do something, according to our gifts.

"What will my friends and neighbors think if I start getting all involved with global concerns?"

They'll think everything from, "Whatever happened to Mary? She used to be so easy-going," to, "Wow! That Mary really has come alive. You should talk to her!"

But there is a more important question. Biblical scholar William Barclay tells the story of a sixteenth-century British pastor preaching in Westminster Abbey when the King of England was in the congregation. The pastor reported thinking to himself, "Latimer, Latimer, be careful what you say. The King of England is here!" Then a voice spoke. "Latimer, Latimer, be careful what you say. The King of Kings is here!" (*Preaching in a Global Context*, 19 February 1989)

A traditional benediction is worth memorizing. "Now may the God of peace, who brought back from the dead our Lord Jesus Christ, the great shepherd of the sheep, by the blood of the eternal covenant, make you complete in everything good so that you may do God's will, working among us that which is pleasing in God's sight, through Jesus Christ, to whom be the glory forever and ever." (Heb. 13:20-21)

In this chapter, we will talk about new ways of feeling, new ways of thinking, new ways of praying, new ways of acting, new ways of celebrating. These areas of our lives are not separate but intricately interwoven. New ways of feeling and thinking may emerge through new ways of acting. New ways of celebrating may bring on new feelings. Praying and acting will certainly occur simultaneously on occasion.

Think of feelings, thoughts, prayers, actions and celebrations as different ways of participating in the common reality of life.

New Ways of Feeling

In relating to a world filled with family members, the direction we must move is captured in such words as solidarity, bridge-building, empathy, reconciliation. But we will understand their meaning only when we see them incarnated, enfleshed, lived out.

We begin with our own lives. Think of times when you or others experienced unfair treatment. When did that first occur and how did you feel? To identify your own feelings is the beginning of global wisdom. Theologian Beverly Wildung Harrison has stated:

> Feeling is the basic bodily ingredient that mediates our connect-edness to the world. When we cannot feel, literally, we lose our connectedness to the world.
>
> All power, including intellectual power, is rooted in feeling. If feeling is damaged or cut off, our power to image the world and act into it is destroyed and our rationality is impaired. But it is not merely the power to conceive the world that is lost. The power to value the world gives way as well.
>
> If we are not perceptive in discerning our feelings, or if we do not know what we feel, we cannot be effective moral agents. (Quoted in *Tales of the Heart*, Tom Hampson and Loretta Whalen, Friendship Press, 1991, p. 20)

New feelings may arise within ourselves as we learn of the experiences of others.

Psychiatrist Robert Coles tells of coming to New York as a medical student, to volunteer at the Catholic Worker house and to meet its director, Dorothy Day. He was shown to the kitchen where Dorothy Day was in conversation with a man of the streets who was obviously deeply disturbed.

> When they had both finished their lunch and their conversation, they got up, and I approached her. She could certainly have guessed that I was going to address her and not her companion. But what she said to me was 'You wanted to speak with one of us . . . ' *With one of us.* Well, that took care of me. I don't think Harvard had anything more to teach me in four years than she had to offer me right then and there. (Originally in the *U.S. Catholic,* reprinted in *Commentary,* edited by Martin Marty, 1 October 1987)

12 STEPS TO THIRD WORLD LIVING

To feel what life is like for much of the world's people, try this exercise of imagination. It is adapted from the U.N. Food and Agriculture Organization's magazine, *Freedom from Hunger*, and based on excerpts from *The Great Ascent* by Robert L. Heilbroner (Harper & Row, New York, 1963).

1. Begin in your house. Take out the furniture: leave a few old blankets, a kitchen table, maybe a wooden chair. You've never had a bed, remember.

2. Throw out your clothes. Each person in the family may keep the oldest suit or dress, a shirt or blouse. The head of the family has the only pair of shoes.

3. All kitchen appliances vanish. Keep a box of matches, a small bag of flour, some sugar and salt, a handful of onions, a dish of dried beans. Rescue those moldy potatoes from the garbage can: those are tonight's meal.

4. Dismantle the bathroom, shut off the running water, take out wiring, lights, everything that runs by electricity.

5. Take away the house; move the family into the toolshed.

6. By now all the other houses in the neighborhood have disappeared. Instead there are shanties, for the fortunate ones.

7. Cancel all the newspapers and magazines. Throw out the books. You won't miss them; you are now illiterate. One radio serves the whole shantytown.

8. No more postman, fireman, government services. The two-classroom school is three miles away. Only two of your seven children attend, and they walk.

9. No hospital, no doctor. The nearest clinic is now 10 miles away with a midwife in charge. You get there by bus or bicycle, if you're lucky enough to have one.

10. Throw out your bankbooks, stock certificates, pension plans, insurance policies. Your cash hoard is now $5.

11. Get out and start cultivating your three acres. Try hard to raise $300 in cash crops because your landlord wants one-third and your money-lender 10 percent.

12. Find some way for your children to bring in a little extra money so that you have something to eat most days. It won't be enough to keep bodies healthy, though, so lop off 25 to 30 years of your life.

New feelings also may come from art and music, from novels and videos. The key is to find those that tell the true story of our global family. Gather some friends and watch the video "El Norte," the story of a brother and sister who, after fleeing military repression in their native Guatemala, struggle to make a new life for themselves as illegal aliens in California. Then talk—not about what you thought, but what you felt.

Have you ever had close relationships with the poor and oppressed? Most of us begin to feel differently if we move from generalized to one-on-one experiences. Some denominations have "Mother-to Mother" programs, in which women from the congregation who are not poor create a community of support with a mother on welfare. In a real sense, the welfare mother is the teacher. The goal is not so much to solve problems (although that happens), but to form friendships and to sense a commonness. Those involved in such programs can no longer caricature or stereotype each other, but recognize that they share the joys, hopes, frustrations, successes and failures of life.

New Ways of Thinking

An old Chinese proverb declares, "Nine-tenths of what we see is behind our eyes." That nine-tenths is called our ideology. What assumptions, conscious and unconscious, are at work in us as we eye the world and its peoples?

Unfortunately, we live in a time of rampant individualism. We are bombarded by advertisements and political messages like, "What's in it for you/me?," "Are you better off than you were five years ago?," "We're #1!," "Those people are taking our jobs!" Every one of us needs to do disciplined thinking if we are to avoid being caught up in unbiblical, life-destroying, "me-first" attitudes. Here are some methods.

1. Study the Bible

Studying the Bible regularly, especially in a community of Christians, will help us move beyond frivolous, superficial ideas. In his brilliant novel, *Darkness at Noon*, Arthur Koestler tells the story of the Communist Party loyalist, Rubashov, who falls out of favor, is arrested, and faces death. In his prison cell, Rubashov recalls that he had really meant to study astronomy but for 40 years had done something else. He muses, "Why had not the Public Prosecutor asked him: 'Defendant Rubashov, what about the infinite?' He would not have been able to answer—and there, there lay the real source of his guilt . . . Could there be a greater?" (Modern Library edition, Random House, New York, 1941, p. 257)

Serious study of the Bible in a community of the concerned will bring us face to face with the infinite and the ultimate.

2. Practice "new thinking"

That's right, practice. Imagine yourself as an attorney presenting the case of the indigenous people of Brazil whose forest home is being destroyed so that others can make a profit and so the government can meet demands imposed by the International Monetary Fund for greater exports. Or, argue the position of the Cree Indian Nation against a hydroelectric power project that will destroy their homes.

State with clarity why indigenous peoples in North and South America did not feel that it was appropriate to celebrate the anniversary of Columbus' "discovery" of America. Or, practice stating the position of an IMF officer who believes that the Fund's requirements for refinancing work for the long-term good of the world's peoples.

Here is another exercise to hone your thinking skills. It was developed by Harvard professor John Rawls, author of *Theory of Justice* (Belknap Press, 1971).

Imagine that you are a member of a small group that has been asked to draw up principles to be followed in the economic system of a just and fair society. As you outline some of these principles, consider how to protect human freedom and how to distribute goods and services fairly. Should they be distributed equally? to each according to her contribution? to each according to his need?

Assume that you know the culture, politics and religion of the society that you are creating, but you do not know what role *you* will have. You may be male or female; rich, poor, or in-between; citizen of a developed or a developing region; healthy or chronically ill; handicapped physically or mentally; member of any ethnic or racial group. Your principles, therefore, must meet the test of fairness/justice from the perspective of all people. Make your notes on the next page.

★

Some principles for a just and fair society:

For Rawls, fairness would occur with the following principles:

- Each person shall have an equal right to liberty compatible with a similar right for all others.

- Some persons will get greater benefits but these should be attached to jobs/positions which are open to all under conditions of equal opportunity.

- Unequal distribution of benefits is just only if it improves the lot of the most disadvantaged.

Rawls' principles have interesting implications for both national and global economic systems, but their greatest value may be in helping us to examine our own lives and ways of thinking.

3. Expose yourself to different sources of information

New thought patterns emerge if our minds are stimulated by new data, or our imaginations are captured by different perspectives. If you don't already, read your denominational magazine; take out a subscription to *Sojourners* or *The Other Side*; get on the mailing list of a human rights organization or UNICEF.

4. Study something new

If you live close to a college or seminary, enroll for a course in Bible or economics or political science or ethics. If taking exams bothers you, just audit the course—but do the work!

★

5. Make international contacts

Invite an international student or
business person into your home for
an evening. Ask questions, listen,
play back what you hear so you're
sure you have understood correctly. Don't argue. If the relationship continues over time, you can
get into a discussion of views that
may differ. At the beginning,
though, most of us need input
more than output.

"Actually, I was hoping for a better return on the Peace Dividend."

6. Ask questions

As we hear different points of view and begin thinking in new ways, we
inevitably start to do social analysis. Michael Czerny and Jamie Swift, in
their very helpful book, *Getting Started on Social Analysis in Canada*, define
social analysis as "a questioning awareness." (Between the Lines Press,
Toronto, Ontario, 1988, p. 14) Social analysis is the habit of asking
"Why?"—of going beyond facts to structures and relationships:

> Why are we creating millionaires at a faster rate than ever before in
> history, while the average family income barely keeps up with
> inflation?

> With the Cold War over, why is there no peace dividend?

> Why have North America and South America developed so differ-
> ently from an economic perspective?

> Why is freer trade enthusiastically supported by some and bitterly
> attacked by others?

> Why does the United States maintain trade barriers against many
> Third World products?

> Why are immigration policies the way they are in the United States
> and Canada?

Such questions lead to more questions. But if we will select an issue of
specific concern to us and pursue those questions in the company of
others, we will begin to analyze not only what has caused the problem
but also what needs to be done to correct it.

7. Take action!

We often act our way into new
thinking. Harvey Cox, whose book
The Secular City prompted wide
discussion when it was published
in 1965, now joins Latin American
thinkers in insisting that action
precedes theological reflection.
Referring to the story of Moses and
the burning bush, Cox writes,
"First hear the Voice, then get to
work freeing the captives. . .
Theology is important but it comes
later." (*The Christian Century*, 7
November 1990, p. 1026)

New Ways of Praying

The most important question to ask as we consider our prayer life is, "What is the nature of the God to whom we pray?" A presidential candidate in the United States announced that his campaign would be built around the theme "America first!" The God who was invoked to bless that campaign is not the God we meet in Jesus Christ. If the Biblical "pointers" we discussed are correct—that God has a vision of Shalom for the whole of creation and a particular concern for the oppressed—then our prayers cannot be for *us* to be better off than *them*. In prayer, we will lift up the aches and the agonies, the joys and the victories of all God's people. Prayer that should widen our vision has too often been used to narrow our perspective.

In our prayers as global Christians, we will do well to remember the people of a specific part of the world. Many denominations have prayer calendars that describe the church's staff and partner churches around the world. Pray not only for your denominational family but also for the whole Christian community and for all the people of each country. Prayer leads us to care more, and want to know more. And knowledge-informed prayer can lead to actions of solidarity.

Christian prayer includes confession about what we have done and what we have failed to do. For most of us, that covers a considerable amount of territory. To the extent that we have, like the rich man dressed in purple and fine linen, lived in abundance and ignored the poor at our gates, we need to confess our lack of sensitivity and action. In Hades, the rich man begged that a message be sent to warn those still on earth. In a sense, many messengers have been sent to us. We are aware of the situation. The biblical judgment is not kind to those who know and still do nothing. The next time you are planning a prayer service, build it around Luke 16:19-31.

Fortunately, as we have discussed earlier, the Christian faith speaks the good news of God's forgiveness. Forgiveness is not a "That's okay, don't worry about it!" transaction. Forgiveness is always available but it calls for repentance and a lively commitment to a changed way of living.

New ways of acting

After you have read through the whole book, review the lists or mural of local, regional and global problems which you developed. Which do you think are the most pressing? Which ones do you think you can affect by your individual behavior and by joining with others to work cooperatively for change? Do you see a global problem that has a local handle? Do you see a local problem which has global ramifications? Pick two or three and strategize how you can work for change. Be sure to assess the actors (people, institutions, corporations) who are key to changing the specific problem. How do power and money relationships need to change? How can you affect this? Work with a partner or small group to strategize. Report back to the larger group. Make some commitments!

To provide a few ideas as "grist" for the mill, below are some actions for both individual and collective action.

1. The next time you are in a small-talk situation, try to work in information or questions about global issues. You may be surprised to discover that other people are interested in more than just their jobs, their children, sports, and the weather. Don't be argumentative; listen to what people have to say. (Baseball player Yogi Berra once said: "How could you get a conversation started in there? Everybody was talking too much!")

2. Recycle. The world's resources have limits. Get your congregation involved in recycling. Sensitizing ourselves and others to the vastly wasteful consumer economy we live in is as important as re-using the materials. If you are feeling quite ambitious, gather a few allies and see if a curbside recycling program exists in your community or if you can get one started. You will quickly learn about social analysis and local politics, skills that can be applied to a number of problems.

3. Start a "5 minutes for peace and justice" program in your church. Ask for five minutes during Sunday service, or space in the form of a bulletin insert. Try to develop a regular schedule (weekly, biweekly, monthly), to highlight different problems or issues. Give some ideas about what people can do. Form a team of people to help.

4. Write to your denominational headquarters and ask what educational materials on global education are available for children and youth. Buy samples and persuade the appropriate church school teachers to use them. Even better, read those materials and offer yourself as a resource.

5. Send $25 to UNICEF. That donation will buy 250 kits for oral rehydration therapy, which saves children's lives, and also will put you on the UNICEF mailing list. Then you will receive information that will steadily nourish your new ways of thinking and feeling.

6. Select one issue related to global economic justice and become well informed. Ask your Member of Parliament or Congressional representative for his/her position and for the Prime Minister's or President's position. Check the library for resources.

7. Write a letter to your local newspaper editor. Express appreciation for the coverage of world events, if that is appropriate, or indicate your interest in having more such coverage. Express your opinion on recent developments in foreign aid or free trade.

8. Once a month, have International Day in your home. Select another country and learn what you can about its people and the issues they face. Write to the embassy in Ottawa or Washington for information on the government's position on economic or other issues. Contact church partners there. Prepare the food of that country; listen to its music; learn about its art, and culture; get to know people from there who may live near you. Invite guests and explain how you are trying to live as a global citizen/family.

9. Use your consumer purchasing power. Decide on your issues and then let your pocketbook vote. You may decide not to buy war toys.

Wasteful excess packaging may affect your purchasing patterns in the supermarket. If you feel that a company's employment practices are unfair to women or racial/ethnic minorities, don't buy that company's products, and write to explain why.

You may feel that your buying decisions will have little impact on a corporation's practices, but you might be the start of a mass movement! Meanwhile, recognize that businesses are highly sensitive to the market and even a few letters will raise questions at the corporate headquarters. Making ethical decisions when you spend money will keep you sensitive to the issues of the marketplace.

10. Identify the co-ops in your area—food, service (like a credit union), agriculture, manufacturing—and support them by buying their products or services, joining them, starting one, educating yourself and others about their potential! Check out national and international cooperative networks. Those like SERRV and Pueblo to People give a higher percentage of the profit to the original producer and try to encourage more equitable and sustainable production processes. Coop America offers everything from a mail-order catalogue of cooperatively produced products to a travel service, insurance, etc! (Coop America, 2100 M Street, N.W., Suite 403, P.O. Box 18217, Washington, D.C. 20036.)

11. Become active in the politics of your precinct or riding. This is surprisingly easy. Decide which political party comes closest to representing the values you hold. Make a small financial contribution to that party. Call the area headquarters and say you would like to volunteer some time. As you become active, let the candidates know of your concerns about global justice issues. A relatively small number of people control the policies and actions of the political parties. If you are willing to do some work, you can become part of that group. You won't be invited to the White House in Washington nor to 24 Sussex Drive in Ottawa, but you will begin to exert some influence on the political process.

12. Volunteer to help your congregation plan for World Communion Sunday, or Ten Days for World Development, or One Great Hour of Sharing. When you get permission—volunteers are almost always accepted with gratitude—select people who share your global concerns or might be interested. Emphasize the whole family of God. Order the educational materials prepared for these different events, or write your own, and get them into the church newsletter and Sunday bulletin.

13. Encourage your congregation to sponsor a refugee family. Write to your denominational headquarters to ask how to get started. If another congregation in your community has sponsored a family, find out about their experience. Successful resettlement efforts require that a small group of persons dedicate considerable time and energy for a short space of time. Use this project as a time to educate the congregation about:

— the home country of the family you are sponsoring

—the reasons why they left their homes

—your government's immigration policies.

14. Consider volunteering for mission or ministry in your own country or elsewhere. Write to your denomination telling what skills you have and when you are available. That will start the process. If service elsewhere is not possible, think about your own community. Stepping outside the society and structures you know, to meet and serve others in God's family, may not require traveling a great distance.

15. Organize a work camp for young people in your own or another country through a Council of Churches or your denominational offices. Be sure to involve the congregations from which the young people come. Encourage the congregations to make a financial contribution to the project and to commit a future Sunday for the young people to report on their experience. Such work camps are often pivotal for young people as they sort out their commitments and make occupational decisions.

16. Encourage your congregation to sponsor an economic refugee in your own country. Many people have been reduced to poverty by an unforeseen illness or company layoff. Sometimes they may not have the skills necessary for the available jobs, but sometimes all they need is a supportive community while they get started again. If there is no one like this in your congregation or in your neighborhood, ask your local social work agency.

17. Keep in touch with your Member of Parliament or Congressperson. Keep them informed about issues you care about; keep yourself informed about what they're doing. Express appreciation when they take positions that reflect your global commitments; state why you disagree with positions that do not. It is essential for the democratic process that politicians do not feel that everybody agrees with them or that no one cares how they vote. It's bad politics—and it's bad for their souls!

18. Investigate how much of your tax dollar goes to military spending. There are a variety of organizations in Canada (such as the Ecumenical Coalition for Economic Justice in Toronto) and the USA (Jobs for Peace in Boston, Massachusetts or Citizens for Tax Justice in Washington, D.C.) which can help with information. Hold a church meeting or conversation with friends or family to share what you find out. Discuss the implications and how you would like to see your tax dollars spent! Inform your Member of Parliament or Congress of your opinions.

19. Invest in the future, your own and the world's. Churches in North America began to use investment funds to advance their justice agenda in 1971, when the first shareholder resolution on withdrawal from South Africa was filed with General Motors. That movement continues through ecumenically coordinated channels in Canada and the United States.

But individuals also can be involved. If you have money to invest, do your own "screening." Decide what corporate practices concern you and avoid those companies that don't measure up to your standards. Screens include doing business in South Africa; involvement with tobacco, alcohol, and gambling, or military weapons, or nuclear power. Other things you might want to check are product quality; environmental performance; community involvement; employment policies. Write to the companies in your portfolio and ask your questions!

Or, you may want to consider a mutual fund that has done the screening for you. A list of such funds, indicating what screens are being used, is available from:

Interfaith Center for Corporate Responsibility
475 Riverside Drive, Room 566
New York, NY 10115-0050

Taskforce on the Churches &
Corporate Responsibility
129 St. Clair Ave. West
Toronto, Ontario, M4V 1N5

Both of these organizations have excellent resources for Christians concerned about the policies and practices of business corporations. For those concerned about risk (a legitimate question for any investment), studies show that ethical restraints seem to have little effect on stock performance. Indeed, some of the mutual funds that attend to social responsibility have consistently out-performed stocks of major corporations.

An additional way in which nearly all of us can be involved in socially responsible investing is through our retirement or life insurance programs. The money which underwrites such programs is invested and we have every right to know what criteria are being used by those who manage these vast sums. Decide how you want to have your pension and/or life insurance funds invested and communicate your ideas to the fund managers. These funds are now large enough to have major impact on corporate practices.

One investment opportunity guarantees a return. Since 1987, the Ecumenical Development Cooperative Society (EDCS) of the World Council of Churches in Geneva has used funds of churches and individuals to make loans for projects which are cooperatively owned and operated by the poor. EDCS reports that its $48 million investment has created more than 7,000 new permanent jobs and directly benefited 500,000 people. The repayment rate of EDCS loans is an astonishing 83 percent. While most of the money has come from denominational investments, individuals may also invest in increments of $250. The financial return is about 2 percent, although a higher rate of interest is available for large contributions. However, making it possible for the poor to help themselves is the greatest return on your investment.

20. Evaluate the environmental and economic consequences of your eating habits. How much meat do you eat? How much of the produce is grown locally? How much produce is in season? Do you buy organic produce or meat? Read *Diet for A Small Planet* by Francis Lappé Moore or *Diet for a New America* by John Robbins.

21. Encourage your church youth group to host a Global Meal. Plan an evening centered on a study of world hunger. When it is time to eat, without advance warning and without comment, serve an excellent meal to two or three of the young people and a small bowl of rice to all the rest. Silverware goes with the full meal; the rest get nothing. See what happens when they experience the world as it really is. After the meal, help them talk about how they felt. Share some information about world hunger. (*Hunger 1992* is a report on world hunger available from your bookstore or from Bread for the World, 802 Rhode Island Ave. N.E., Washington, D.C. 20018.)

22. Take a "purposeful tour" or "responsible vacation." Too many tours isolate the members from the realities of the local situation. Some denominations sponsor tours to countries where they have overseas staff or partner churches. Some human rights groups organize issue-oriented trips.

A number of organizations offer exposure visits or cross-cultural experiences, to enable North Americans to understand something about the life of the poor. Global Awareness Through Experi-

ence (GATE) has a study center in Mexico City which offers a one- or two-week group learning experience with frequent field trips, informative lectures, and time for worship and reflection. Write to GATE, 936 Winnebago St., LaCrosse, WI 56401. The Lutheran Center for Global Education features residential and travel seminars in Mexico, Central and South America, the Caribbean, the Philippines, Southern Africa and the Middle East. Write to Augsburg College, 731 21st St. South, Minneapolis, MN 55454.

23. Form a group or join one already in existence to look at the links between poverty and racism in your community. Meet with a variety of individuals and groups who can help enrich your understanding of what's involved. What alliances between white people and people of color need to be established or strengthened to work on this issue? What can be done locally, regionally, nationally? Have members of your group commit to take concrete actions to work on the issues.

24. Volunteer your time to work with those who have been maimed,

limited or ignored by our society. The needs are almost endless. You can assist in a shelter for homeless men or women, teach reading or English as a second language, serve as a volunteer parole officer, help at a home for battered women, spend time with AIDS patients, join your community's emergency help system.

Volunteering of time and money is a generous fact of life in North America. A Gallup Survey in the United States showed that in 1990, 98.4 million people volunteered their time, a 23 percent increase over 1988. They put in 20.5 billion hours with a dollar value of $170 billion. An estimated 100 million people contributed money. Interestingly, those with annual family incomes of under $10,000 gave 5.5 percent of their income to others while those making $50,000 gave only 1.7 percent. Those who support their churches regularly are also the leaders in supporting other causes. (Gallup Survey, 1990). Robert Payton, the first professor of Philanthropic Studies at the University of Indiana, says that voluntarism is "at the very heart of democracy . . . You're doing it for some good larger than yourself."

And you thought there was nothing you could do!

The story is told of a famous monastery that had fallen on hard times. The monastery stood in a beautiful setting near a wood. But the monks who had once busied themselves with work and prayer were now few in number and went about gloomy and dispirited. Occasionally their boredom was interrupted when they saw a rabbi visiting a small hut near the edge of the wood.

One day, the abbot of the monastery decided to share his problems with the rabbi. Invited into the little hut, he told the rabbi about the discouraging condition of the monastery. The rabbi said, "I will give you a teaching, but it can only be repeated once. After that, no one must ever say it aloud again." Then the rabbi looked at the abbot and said, "The Messiah is among you." Silently the abbot returned to the monastery and the next day he gathered the monks together.

"I went yesterday to visit the rabbi," he told them. "He gave me a story, a lesson, but it must be spoken only once and never again." Then he looked at each monk, one by one, and said "The Messiah is among you." The monks were startled. What could it mean? Was it Brother John, or Paul, or Alexander? Each wondered, "Am I the Messiah?"

They began to treat one another with reverence, with gentleness and caring. Soon the monastery was echoing with the joyous singing of Gregorian chants. The people of the neighborhood began to come again, nourished by the spirit they saw among the monks. Soon the people began to treat each other differently, too. Believing the Messiah was among them changed their lives.

In your volunteering, it is important always to remember that inasmuch as you have done it to one of the least, you have done it unto the Christ.

New Ways of Celebrating

It is easy to be discouraged. The suffering in our world is great and the problems do seem intractable. But as Christians we are called upon to celebrate the good news that life is always overcoming death. Knowing our own self-centeredness, we should not be surprised that injustice walks the planet. What is truly astonishing is that persons of good will, in every corner of the world, driven by a divine discontent, stand up against it. That is worth celebrating.

In our churches we give considerable attention to liturgy, which literally means "the work of the people." Following this train of thought, one might consider the work of the people of God as they live out their daily lives as the "Major Liturgy." The order of worship, then, would be the "Minor Liturgy." Our liturgy should be an empowering celebration of our need to give thanks, to confess and to hear the message of forgiveness, to listen to the word of God that redirects us, to make again an act of commitment, and then to leave in order to serve.

In most of this chapter, we have urged that a global consciousness inform our feelings, our thoughts, our prayers and our actions. Equally important, our worship must affirm the whole family of God. To do otherwise is to shrink the gospel, domesticate the good news, privatize the faith.

The celebration of communion or Holy Eucharist is an opportunity to lift up the centrality of a global vision. This is not our table, it is Christ's table. The invitation comes not from us but from Christ. And if the "least ones" of the world are not gathered there with us, even symbolically, then we must ask ourselves whether or not we have excluded Christ.

We have many ways to keep our celebrations world-centered. The use of another language—for example, Spanish in the United States, French in Canada—will remind us that we are to be bridge-builders across the chasms that separate us. Special Sundays can celebrate the traditions of the Christian community in different cultures. Prayers can be lifted up for specific countries or even for specific persons—a political prisoner, a church leader witnessing with faith and courage (Lutheran Bishop Medardo Gomez in El Salvador comes to mind), an unknown mother in Zambia or a street child in Brazil.

As Paul exhorted the Hebrews, "Since we are receiving a kingdom that cannot be shaken, let us give thanks, by which we offer to God an acceptable worship with reverence and awe." (Heb. 12:28) That will happen best if we are joined in worship with our sisters and brothers around the world.

A Last Word or Two
If Not Us, Who? If Not Now, When?

Neither the author nor the readers of this workbook have become experts in the field of global economics. Many items were not discussed—international currency exchange, labor unions, globally interdependent stock markets, Special Drawing Rights of the IMF, the Import-Export Bank or the Canadian Wheat Board, the use and abuse of immigrant laborers, the complex issues in an unsettled Eastern Europe, to name a few.

But we have begun to look at what theologian Reinhold Niebuhr says is the first ethical question: "What's going on out there?" And as we have explored the meaning of our Christian commitment to the world, we have begun answering another question: "What's going on in here?" We must continue on both the inner journey and outer journey.

Teacher and preacher William Willimon states the matter well:

> True faith, the kind to which Jesus calls us, is the assurance of things hoped for, the conviction of things not seen. It is a process, not a possession. It gives us something to chew on for the rest of our lives. Faith is certitude in the midst of doubt, rather than certainty with no doubts. Faith is a journey with a compass which points us in the right direction, not a detailed map which tells us every step to take. Faith is not being sure where you are going, but going anyway because you like the travelling companions and you know who leads the way. Faith is a journey which you do not wait to begin until you are desperate and have nowhere else to go, or until you are devastated and miserable and are forced to go; faith is going because you have heard the good news that the Guide is trustworthy and that the trip is worth the cost.

If you have not tried to act in solidarity with the worldwide family of God before, you may feel anxious or even afraid. Knowing about others who have lived through just such an experience can be helpful.

If Not Here, Where?

An 80-year-old woman made her first trip to Central America in 1991 as part of a purposeful tour of church women. Lutheran Archbishop Medardo Gomez of El Salvador told them, "It's dangerous to be here. You must be the crazy people of God." As she visited with persons who daily risked their lives, she lost heart.

> I sit in the the comfort of my pew; they were in danger of their lives for teaching and preaching the simple gospel to heal the sick, to comfort the comfortless, to help people become whole persons in Christ. . . I never had the courage to wear a cross in El Salvador. People have been shot for doing that. . . Slowly as the days went by, I realized I was no longer afraid. Something of these people's courage became a part of me. Something of their unshakeable faith took hold and deepened mine. . . In Central America the gospel is heavy to carry, but gradually you realize that the gospel carries you. (Disciples of Christ report)

The good news of God found through Jesus Christ allows us to get started and continue the journey with quiet confidence.

A few years ago, the displays at the New York Botanical Gardens were housed under large glass domes. You traveled from one to the next through tunnels which were absolutely dark. Naturally, you approached the entrances with a slight sense of apprehension. But at the entrance to each of the tunnels was a small sign which read: "The light will come on when you step into the darkness."

Anyone who has even a minimal knowledge of what is involved in working for justice in an interdependent world will approach that assignment with some apprehension too. There is a lot of darkness out there. But as we take that first step forward, a light comes on and our experience-tested faith affirms that "the darkness cannot overcome it."

Is it possible to live as a Christian global citizen, as a member of the worldwide family of Christ? It certainly is! Risky? Sometimes. Exciting? You better believe it! Satisfying? Incredibly so! Demanding? Totally! And most importantly, faith-full, for we come in the name of the one who brought good news to the poor.

So, the end is just the beginning?

66

IDEAS FOR GROUP LEADERS

Before you begin leading a study of a Christian approach to global economics, you must know the answers to certain questions. These include the five W's of journalism fame: who, what, where, when and why.

- Who will be in your group?
- What do they know? What do they want to learn?
- Where will they meet? When? How often?
- Why do they want to be in the group? Do they have a particular concern, or a generalized interest?

Members of groups vary widely in terms of their present knowledge, their willingness to prepare for the sessions, their current point of view and their openness to new ideas, their ability to participate in group discussions. You will have to decide how to lead the group and organize the sessions based on the people and the time frame.

Identify your main goal for this study, and theirs: To learn new information? To change deep-seated feelings about the "enemy," the "other?" To motivate people to act? To encourage a fresh way of looking at the world as we watch television, listen to the radio and read the papers? To re-think how the Christian faith relates to such worldly matters as economics and politics? Prioritize the group's goals, and plan your study with those goals in mind. A number of possible approaches are suggested below. Be sure to order needed resources such as the videos *A Matter of Interest* or *The Debt Crisis: An Unnatural Disaster*, well ahead of time.

1. Ask the members to describe how they have experienced or recognized the economic interdependence of our world. This sharing could move rather quickly from a somewhat casual "All my

kids' toys are made in Hong Kong" to an emotion-filled "My spouse no longer has a job. The factory moved to Mexico for cheap labor. They gave us one month's notice." Feelings need to be surfaced and affirmed. We have different reactions to global economic realities depending upon our experiences.

2. Use the world problems exercise on page 3 and/or the home and personal effects exercise on page 4. Ask the members to read illustrations of our global interrelationships in this book (pp 60-65 on freer trade vs. more protectionism, or p. 90 on "Twelve Steps to Third World Living"), or bring in examples of others.

3. The Biblical material in Part 2 is best used in small discussion groups. Divide your group into clusters of two or three persons, and assign each cluster one of the six sets of Biblical passages. (It would be good to do this at the end of one week's session, so that members can read the material before the next week's session. Let each small group consider how its particular Biblical pointer might affect their thinking and acting. Gather the whole group together, and discuss all six Biblical pointers. Do people feel they are all valid? Are there others?

4. Plan a discussion on how people make decisions about right and wrong. Begin with sharing in small groups. Then use the case studies in Part 2 (pp 32-37), or make up some of your own, as a way of discerning how to move from the general to the specific, from "love of God and neighbor" to "What do I do when?" Let the group talk about whether the four approaches cited—rule, prayer, situational ethics, middle axioms—are helpful in making ethical choices. If not, what other ways can we use to make such decisions?

IDEAS FOR GROUP LEADERS

5. The economics material in Parts 3 and 4 may be new for most group members. Some possibilities for presenting these ideas are:

A) Use the family budget building exercise (pp. 43-45) to illustrate basic economic concepts such as unlimited wants, scarcity, opportunity costs, decisions at the margin. Or, it might be appropriate to build a church or outreach program budget.

B) Briefly explain traditional and command economies (pp. 47-48). Then have the group set prices for the garage sale (page 49). How are prices set by the market? Discuss the factors which influence the economic role of women in traditional, command and market economies.

C) If a college is nearby, ask someone from the economics department to discuss the basic notions involved. Emphasize the need for group involvement and simple illustrative material to help the average non-economist understand and use these concepts.

D) Discuss what goals we have for the economic system of our country. How does the Christian faith relate to these goals? Use the John Rawls exercise (pp. 91-92) as another way of thinking about a just economic system.

E) Some groups will be able to have a lively discussion on the Canada-U.S. Free Trade Agreement. That discussion needs to be more than an "I like it—I don't like it" debate. What criteria does our faith provide for evaluating trade arrangements?

F) Assign group members the roles of the people described on p. 60. Discuss the advantages and disadvantages of freer trade. Then summarize the pro and con arguments described on pages 61-65.

G) Use the Third World debt quiz (p. 67) as an entry into the international debt crisis. There is nothing wrong with short lectures to provide information. Canadian and U.S. citizens need to understand that current repayment policies, which both governments support, are having a devastating effect on the most vulnerable people throughout the developing world.

H) Plan to use the video *A Matter of Interest*, which offers a short lively narrative of the debt crisis, or another video. See the box on page 109.

I) A group able to spend two hours in one session can have a great time with *Caribbean Money-Go-Round*, a simulation game created by Patricia Brady to teach global economics through Caribbean realities. Players take roles of farmers, fishermen, garment workers, a businessman or Navy lieutenant, and Christian aid and non-governmental development organizations, and must make difficult choices for survival as various events occur. Available at $19.95 from Friendship Press. (For more information, see inside of back cover, "Caribbean Debt Game.")

J) Ask group members to interpret foreign aid, Third World debt or the role of multinational corporations from the perspective of one of the persons listed on (pages 73-74). The effectiveness of impersonations will depend on the participants briefing themselves thoroughly before they begin. Brief statements by the group members in their various roles can be followed by a general discussion. Don't forget to focus on what insights the Christian faith provides on the issues.

6. All or part of your group's study of global economics could be centered on one of the action proposals in Part 5, pages 95-98, or any other project the group (or the congregation) may undertake. Sometimes the best thinking takes place as we reflect on some action we have taken or some project in which we are engaged. Your group might take leadership in resettling a refugee family, or examining where your church's investment funds are placed, or beginning a church recycling program, or planning a World Communion Sunday.

IDEAS FOR GROUP LEADERS

Group action projects often get bogged down because a few simple organizational procedures are not followed. If you decide to act, use this checklist.

A) Get group agreement on the project.

B) Select a project that can really be done. That is, be realistic but stretch yourselves.

C) Define precisely what you want to do and how you will know when it has been done.

D) Make concrete plans and specific assignments with a timeline for completion.

E) Let each person know that she/he will get a call from time to time to see how things are going.

F) Evaluate as you go and make necessary changes in methods and assignments, or even goals.

G) Decide when the project has been completed and have a party. We need to celebrate even small victories.

H) Return to Step A. There are lots of other actions worth taking on!

7. Use the resources in your own community to study about global economics: international college students or faculty, business leaders, economists, community organizers (issues in our inner cities are not unlike those of the Third World). But don't just "get a speaker." Be very clear about the subject matter to be covered (be specific, not generic), and insist that group members be involved in discussing the issues raised.

8. Do not forget learnings that can come from experiencing a taste of other cultures—their music and art, their foods, their stories and legends. Begin with international people in your congregation or community. Your denomination's overseas division may be able to offer international visitors. Your public library may have information; your local school system may have names. UNICEF (United Nations Plaza, 44th Street at First Avenue, New York, NY 10017) has excellent materials. Or, write to the embassies of countries in which you have a special interest.

Using these eight suggestions, a six-session study might look like this:
    Session 1—Ideas 1, 2 and 3
    Session 2—Idea 4
    Session 3—Ideas 5A, B and D: or 5C
    Session 4—Ideas 5E; 5F or 5I; 5G; or Idea 7
    Session 5—Idea 6
    Session 6—Idea 8

These are only a few suggestions for ways to approach a very complicated subject. You know your group best. Some groups take study very seriously; others are more casual. Start where your group is. Some will just be starting to realize the implications of the song, "God's got the whole world in his [her] hands." Others will be looking for a way to help solve the global problems that confront us.

Wherever you begin, you'll probably end up in a different place, with everyone realizing in a new way how our lives as Christian people and as citizens of the U.S. or Canada are affected by global economics.

IDEAS FOR GROUP LEADERS

The following exercise was designed by the Women's Division of the United Methodist Church. It is suitable for large groups (20 or more participants), with time for research, discussion and analysis.

Times of Crisis

What in the world is going on?

EXERCISE

Divide into small groups according to geographic regions, such as:
- U.S. & Canada
- Mexico, Caribbean, Central and South America
- "Western" Europe
- The Commonwealth of Independent States and what was formerly "Eastern Europe"
- Asia
- Africa south of the Sahara
- Northern Africa and the Middle East

Have each group develop a list on newsprint of what they think are the major challenges (political, economic, social) facing each region or a few countries in each region. Can you identify some economic linkages with challenges you might first see as more political or social? Report back to the entire group. Identify similar issues among the regions. What are important differences? Where are interconnections in the causes and consequences of these problems between regions or specific countries? Be sure to analyze the problems in your local area for comparison.

You may want to draw your reports and group analysis out in a mural fashion. This can enable you to see the global and regional pictures and trace out linkages more easily than by making lists. (A very popular mural drawing technique has been developed by the Ecumenical Coalition for Economic Justice, 11 Madison Avenue, Toronto, Ontario, Canada M5R2S2. (416) 921-4615. It is described in a short paperback book *Ah-Hah!: A New Approach to Popular Education*.)

THE STATE OF THE WORLD IN A NUTSHELL

- There are about 1.2 billion poor people in the developing nations of the South. This number is expected to rise about 10% by 2000.
- By the year 2000, the bulk of the poor will live in Africa, rather than in Asia, as they do presently.
- Global distribution of income is very skewed: 77% of the world's people earn only 15% of its income.
- People in the North earn on average $12,510—18 times the average in the South, $710.
- The net flow of resources from North to South has reversed. During 1980-81 about $21 billion a year in net aid, loans and investments were channeled from highly affluent nations of the North to the South. By 1984, more money was flowing South to North (as debt repayments, royalties to multinational corporations, etc.). Between 1984-89, a net $241 billion poured into the North. There is no indication that this trend is abating.
- Wars and military expenditures take a heavy social and economic toll. During the Gulf War, for example, Jordan lost 40% of its Gross National Product because of lost trade and worker's remittances.
- Non-oil exporting developing nations' share of world trade declined between 1968-88. Future prospects are poor for those not associated with major trading blocs in the Pacific Basin (dominated by Japan), Western Europe or North America.
- "Significant environmental degradation is usually caused by poverty in the South—and by affluence in the North . . . Three-quarters of the poor people in the South live in ecologically fragile zones, and around 14 million have become environmental refugees—driven from their homes by ecological degradation."
- "The average person in the South consumes only one-third of the energy resources consumed by a person in the North." This means that the 20% of the world's population who live in the North produces about 50% of the world's greenhouse gases.

(From United Nations Development Program, *Human Development Report 1991*, Oxford University Press, pp. 22-29.)

IDEAS FOR GROUP LEADERS

THE STATE OF THE WORLD IN A NUTSHELL

The following is a brief overview of some critical problems in a few areas of the world:

Sub-Saharan Africa:

■ GNP per capita fell an average of 2.2% annually during the 1980s.

■ Mortality rates for children under 5 are 178 per 1,000 live births. This is more than three times the rate for Southeast Asia and over double the rate for Latin America and the Caribbean. In some countries, such as Angola, Mali, Mozambique, Malawi and Sierra Leone, 25% or more of the children die before they are 5.

■ More than half the population has no access to public health services.

■ About two-thirds of the people lack safe water.

■ An estimated 100 million are unemployed in 1989. This is four times the number in 1979. Unemployment is concentrated among women and young men. Another 100 million are "underemployed" (not full time; not fully using skills).

■ Real wages (wages adjusted for inflation) fell 30% between 1980-89.

■ "By 1989, a combination of apartheid, social unrest and military skirmishes had created about 6 million refugees and 50 million disabled persons. Including the effects of natural disasters and difficult socio-economic conditions adds another 35 million displaced people."

■ "The outlook for Africa is bleak unless concerted national and international efforts set the continent on a more positive course." Without this, more than half the continent's population will fall below the poverty line by 2000.

(From UNDP *Human Development Report 1991*, pp. 35-36.)

Latin America and the Caribbean:

■ "The economic problems of the 1980s have hit this region hard. The debt crisis, high interest rates, barriers raised against Latin American exports and low commodity prices—all have wrought havoc with some of the region's past achievements in human development."

■ "Average inflation rates soared above 100% during the 1980s in Argentina, Bolivia, Brazil and Peru—eroding real wages and discouraging investment."

■ Employment has shifted towards less productive activities in the informal sector where there are no employment protections or guarantees like pensions, sick leave, etc.

■ Productivity and living standards fell during the 1980s.

■ Child malnutrition and infant mortality started to rise in many countries.

■ Income distribution remains very highly skewed in many countries. In Peru, the bottom 40% of the population earns 13% of the national income. This is far worse than in India, for example, where this segment earns 20%. In Brazil, the top 20% of the population earns 26 times more than the bottom 20%.

■ Some of the poorest countries have very inadequate social services and infrastructure. In Haiti, Bolivia, El Salvador and Paraguay, less than one-half the population has access to safe water.

(From UNDP, *Human Development Report 1991*, p. 34.)

IDEAS FOR GROUP LEADERS

THE STATE OF THE WORLD IN A NUTSHELL

South Asia:

■ Asia is one of the poorest regions of the world. GNP per capita remains very low, particularly in Nepal ($180) and Bangladesh ($170).

■ "Inequality is one of the most striking features of South Asia—between rich and poor, males and females, different regions and different ethnic groups. In rural Punjab, landless families have infant mortality levels 36% higher than those for landowning families."

■ "In Asia as a whole, one child in three suffers from malnutrition, and nearly 700 million people live in poverty, with the great majority of them in two countries—India and Bangladesh."

■ One-third of the population does not have access to health services or clean water.

■ "Female life expectancy is low, with a substantial number of women who would have lived if they had been born elsewhere."

(From UNDP *Human Development Report 1991*, pp. 33-34.)

EXERCISE

Return to your lists of major challenges at home and around the world which you constructed in the previous exercise. Where do you see signs of hope? What stories can you tell from your own life, from your family, church and community, where people are working to make a difference? What do you find inspiring? What in the stories of pain and hope challenges you as a Christian? Challenges your church? our society? As a result of sharing these stories and concerns, what economic issues do you want to explore further?

United States:

■ By the end of 1988, an index of the USA's "social health" compiled by Fordham University—designed to measure society's well-being (such as infant mortality rates, children in poverty, unemployment, housing, health care access, etc.)—had dropped nearly in half from the Nixon-Ford era. 56 ～ 62

■ Fordham University's social index analysis found that the decline in the quality of life for Americans was borne disproportionately among women. Moreover, women of color were most hurt by the socio-economic decline of the 1980s.

■ The buying power of hourly wages fell more than 9% between 1980 and 1989. Working people's average benefits fell by nearly 14% in this period.

■ The income disparity in the U.S. has grown dramatically. Between 1977 and 1990, the top 1% of the population (who earn more than $549,000 annually) saw their after-tax income grow by 110%, while those with incomes below $44,900 saw theirs decline by 7-14%.

■ Nearly 36 million people are poor, according to the most recent U.S. Census Bureau estimates for 1991. Over 14 million of them are children and young people under 18. This translates into the fact that about one in every five children is poor.

■ The national debt rose from $73.8 billion in 1980 to $3 trillion in 1991.

[From *Reaganomics and Women: Structural Adjustment U.S. Style—1980-1992. A Case Study of Women and Poverty in the U.S.* Alternative Women-In-Development working group, Center of Concern, Washington, D.C., 1992.)

Visualize the Debt Crisis

The 13-minute video *A Matter of Interest* offers a useful, lively way to understand the international debt crisis. Factors that have set off, expanded and deterred repayment of debts incurred by Third World nations are explained using an animated format.

Plan to order this video (see **Filmography**, page 117) and view it as a group. Because the video is short, you may decide to show it at more than one point—for example, to introduce world economic issues or to focus on Third World debt during your study of Part 4 of this book.

1. Preview this audiovisual to acquaint yourself with the contents and to check your equipment. Plan a discussion based on the suggestions here or on your own questions. For a more extensive discussion, see the study guide packaged with the video.

2. Before showing *A Matter of Interest*, ask participants to:

A. List some ways in which they experience debt and the causes of that debt; or

B. List questions from their reading of Part 4 about the causes, consequences and possible solutions of Third World debt. (Use newsprint or chalkboard for the list.)

3. View the video.

4. Discuss the video.

A. Ask the group to work in pairs or threes to diagram the sequence of events that led the people of Brazico into debt (supply paper and pencils). After about 10 minutes, come together to share the results. Devise a group chart incorporating the ideas. It might look like this:

Oil price quadruples → Western banks lend to Third World borrowers at low interest rates → US economic policy forces up interest rates → Higher rates plus decline in prices of Third World resources lead to repayment problems → Banks promise more time to pay if Brazico will accept IMF conditions → New loans are made available → Brazico owes more money for a longer period

List those responsible for Brazico's debt crisis.

B. In what ways does Maisy Mills' predicament resemble that of Brazico's? Are the causes of a country's debt comparable to those of the debt of an individual? If you made a list for 2A above, look at those responses again here. What about your own country's debt? How large is it? To whom is it owed? How will it be repaid? How is it similar to and different from Brazico's debt? How does it affect the issues of Third World debt?

C. If you listed questions in 2B above, see which questions the video has helped to answer and which ones remain. How will your group go about finding further answers?

D. As a group, list some solutions that have been proposed. These could include economic reforms within debtor countries; investment in Third World economies so that they can "grow" their way out of debt; "debt swaps" in which lenders "sell" devalued debts for shares of companies or government bonds in debtor countries; reduction of debts—sometimes with guarantees of repayment of lower debts and economic reforms; refusal to pay; regulations to recover capital flight; cancellation of debts.

Which solutions seem to make the best economic sense? Which solutions make ethical sense, according to principles group members consider important? Are there solutions that combine economic sense with important ethical principles? Remember the groups affected by any resolution: people in Third World countries, governments of those countries, lender banks, international cooperative lending organizations, people in industrialized countries and governments of industrialized countries.

To explore the issues of Third World debt in an actual setting, show *The Debt Crisis: An Unnatural Disaster* (see **Filmography**, page 118). In this longer video, Caribbean people look at how their countries' debts affect their lives. As they work at understanding the causes, they also seek solutions that will allow them to become more self-sufficient. Many of the questions above can be adapted for this video, or you can use the study guide packaged with it.

BIBLIOGRAPHY

This bibliography offers a select sampling from the multitude of books recently published on global economics and related issues.

Look for these and other resources in church, community and college libraries, local bookstores, and denominational resource centers. Please do not order them from Friendship Press. Also, please note that prices and availability of books may change.

Resources of related interest from Friendship Press are listed on the inside back cover of this book. Please note that the "Caribbean Debt Game" has been re-titled "Caribbean Money-Go-Round." Audiovisual resources are listed in the **Filmography** which follows this section.

Most denominations in Canada and the United States, as well as ecumenical agencies and consortia, have issued study or policy papers on some aspects of global economics. These are available from denominational offices. The Roman Catholic Bishops in the U.S. and Canada have published position papers analyzing the economic issues in their respective countries.

Information regarding the positions of the governments of the United States or Canada with regard to trade, International Monetary Fund policies, and other global economic issues, may be obtained from your Congressional representatives or Members of Parliament.

Friendship Press is grateful to the Women's Division, General Board of Global Ministries, United Methodist Church, for assistance with this listing.

Economic Theory

A Woman's Collective Project. *Learning Economics: Empowering Women for Action.* New York: The Religious Network for Equality for Women, 1992. One facilitator's guide and one participant packet, $13.00.

Two large paperback books make up this six-session economic literacy program designed to help women understand how their personal economic situations connect with those of other women and to the economy as a whole. One session on inter-

national business is entitled, "The Journey of the Blouse." Companion video available.

Cavanagh, John and John Gershman, Karen Baker, Gretchen Helmke, eds. *Trading Freedom: How Free Trade Affects Our Lives, Work and Environment.* San Francisco: Institute for Food and Development Policy, 1992. $10.00.

Thirty contributors from Canada, Mexico and the U.S. challenge the false promises of free trade in the Americas, outline an ambitious alternative vision, and present concrete strategies to build an integrated North America based on the principles of ecological sustainability, equity, social justice and democracy.

Dowd, Douglas. *The Waste of Nations: Dysfunction in the World Economy.* Boulder: Westview Press, 1989. $16.95.

Capitalist systems use waste to maintain profits by creating scarcity, Dowd says. Excess packaging, planned obsolescence, military build-up and underutilized labor, all examples of planned waste, have put the world economy in crisis. Dowd offers a plan for change in economic and social policy, a new kind of capitalism which reduces the military and alleviates exploitation.

Enloe, Cynthia. *Beaches, Bananas and Bases: Making Feminist Sense of International Politics.* Berkeley: University of California Press, 1990. $12.95.

A lively treatment of women's roles in the global economy and international politics. Enloe writes in an easy and engrossing way.

Epping, Randy Charles. *A Beginner's Guide to the World Economy: Seventy-One Basic Concepts That Will Change the Way You See the World.* New York: Vintage Press, 1992. $10.00.

Epping answers questions such as, What is the European Community? Where did the Third World debt come from? What is GNP? How do communist countries make the transition to capitalism? This book can be used like an encyclopedia, but is written with humor and simplicity.

Lustig, Nora. *North American Free Trade: Assessing the Impact*. Washington, DC: Brookings Institute, 1992. $10.95.

Morici, Peter. *Making Free Trade Work: The Canada-U.S. Agreement*. Washington, DC: Council of Foreign Affairs, 1990. $17.95.

Morici, Peter. *A New Special Relationship: Free Trade and U.S.-Canada Economic Relations in the 1990s*. Ashgate Publishing Company, 1991. $23.95.

Both of these books present a positive view of free trade but raise critical questions about its implications.

Reich, Robert. *The Work of Nations*. New York: Vintage, 1992. $12.00.

Reich, the leading economist for the Clinton administration, explains there is no such thing as an American economy, with "national" corporations or industries. Rather, Reich sees a world economy and he asks, "What are the skills, products and services needed for the 21st century? How can all citizens of the U.S. and the world share in this new global economy?" Reich's solution to world problems is to see each country's primary assets as its citizen's skills and insights.

Swift, Jamie and Brian Tomlinson, eds. *Conflicts of Interest*. Toronto: Between the Lines, 1991.

A critical analysis of the Canadian government's policies vis à vis the Third World.

Thurow, Lester. *Dangerous Currents*. New York: Vintage Books, 1984. $7.95.

Intended to be a layperson's guide to understanding popular economic theories, this book explains supply-side economics and why we should care about the currents that affect our course, nationally and internationally.

Vickers, Jeanne. *Women and the World Economic Crisis*. Atlantic Highlands, NJ: Zed Books, 1991. $15.95.

The world economic crisis is a result of international debt. Women did not create this problem and yet women and their children throughout the world are forced to pay the debt back. The book uses short articles, photographs, cartoons, charts and case studies on five developing countries. Vickers explains how to build solidarity and co-responsibility.

Wright, Robin and Doyle McManus. *Flashpoints: Promise and Peril in a New World*. New York: Alfred A. Knopf, 1991. $24.00.

These two journalists visited hot spots all over the world and came away celebrating the prospects for democracy, but also viewed a new world "disorder" and disintegration. After the decline of the Cold War, they see trends such as a North-South gap in development, over against an East-West difference; economic strength becoming more important than military clout; ethnic, nationalist and fundamentalist movements causing conflicts within communities; massive human migrations resulting in racism; and international environmental and health problems.

Global Industry

Fuentes, Annette and Barbara Ehrenreich. *Women in the Global Factory*. Boston: South End Press, 1983. $5.00.

This book looks at women on the global assembly line in countries that U.S. businesses exploit in order to take advantage of tax-free, union-free and unregulated markets. Fuentes and Ehrenreich examine the economic and political forces which allow women to be paid between $3 and $5 per day. The book also describes ways women organize themselves around the world.

Kamel, Rachael. *The Global Factory*. Philadelphia: American Friends Service Committee, 1990. $7.50.

An easy way to understand a complex subject. By looking at plant closings, U.S. factories in Mexico and labor unions in the Philippines, this book teaches about global economics and economic exploitation, with a special focus on women. Kamel emphasizes the need for a coalition to work for justice.

Lowe, Janet. *The Secret Empire: How Twenty-Five Multi-Nationals Rule the World*. Homewood, IL: Business 1 Irwin, 1992. $24.95.

A critical but balanced look at the largest of the world's multinational corporations, by a journalist specializing in economic issues.

Ogle, George. *South Korea: Dissent Within the Economic Miracle*. Highland: Zed Humanities Press, 1990. $17.50.

A look behind the popular notion that Asian nations such as Korea, Taiwan and Singapore have undergone "economic miracles" and represent models of development for the rest of the world. Ogle examines the social and political costs of these economic policies.

Ward, Kathryn, ed. *Women Workers and Global Restructuring*. Ithaca: ILR Press, 1990. $14.95.

Scholarly essays discuss the global assembly line which forces women in less privileged countries to do the manufacturing work for the privileged countries. The essays describe the socio-economic positions of women in developing countries, and emphasize that employers use gender- and race-specific tactics to control women.

Global Debt

Barton, Carol and Barbara Weaver. *The Global Debt Crisis: A Question of Justice*. Washington, DC: Interfaith Foundation, 1989. $4.00.

This workbook sparks discussion and action on the international debt crisis. From a faith perspective, the book encourages reflection on issues of hunger and poverty in the world and built into world economic systems. Bible studies, testimonies, resources and a leader's guide are included for creating five study sessions on the global economy.

Debt Crisis Network. *A Journey through the Global Debt Crisis*. Washington, DC: Institute for Policy Studies/ Transnational Institute.

Comic-book style, basic and lively description of the major players in the crisis. Lends itself to role play.

George, Susan. *A Fate Worse Than Debt*. New York: Evergreen Books, 1988. $9.95.

Information on Third World debt collected from grassroots organizations. George maintains that "economic policies are not neutral," and emphasizes that debt concerns everyone on this planet. Major attention is given to Africa, the poorest of all continents, South America, and ecological disasters. (See also *How the Other Half Dies*.)

George, Susan. *The Debt Boomerang: How Third World Debt Harms Us All*. London: Pluto Press with the Transnational Institute, 1992.

Examines six ways in which the Third World "debt boomerang" strikes the North as it flies back from the South. These "debt connections" are environmental destruction, drugs, costs to taxpayers, lost jobs and markets, immigration pressures, and heightened conflict and war. Shocking statistics, and a powerful message about why solidarity with the South is not just ethically desirable but in our interest as well.

Nossiter, Bernard D. *The Global Struggle for More: Third World Conflicts with Rich Nations*. New York: Harper & Row, 1987. $22.50.

Mainstream journalist focuses on debt, aid and trade in the North and the South. Nossiter explains the roles and dynamics of GATT, OPEC, IMF and the U.N. Nossiter debunks the American myth that the South corrupts free markets, overturns established banking systems and is suspicious of capitalism in general. He also refutes the belief held by many Asians, Africans and Latin Americans, that industrial countries are rich, miserly and exploitative.

Sustainable Development

Center for Investigative Reporting and Bill Moyers. *Global Dumping Ground: The International Traffic in Hazardous Waste.* Washington, DC: Seven Locks Press, 1990. $11.95.

> The United States is the world leader in the lucrative and scandal-ridden business of disposing of hazardous waste. The complicated problems of dumping in Third World countries, the need to generate less waste, ineffective U.S. policies, mislabeling of hazardous materials, and the high cost of disposal in the U.S., all have few simple solutions.

Leonard, H. Jeffrey, Richard E. Feinferg and Valeriana Kalleb, eds. *Environment and the Poor: Development Strategies for a Common Agenda.* New Brunswick: Transaction Publishers, 1989. $15.95.

> When people are forced to meet their short-term needs, they cannot examine the long-term consequences of their actions. These essays discuss ways to eliminate absolute poverty, slow population growth and safeguard the environment.

McAfee, Kathy. *Storm Signals: Structural Adjustment and Development Alternatives in the Caribbean.* Boston: South End Press and Oxfam America, 1991. $15.00.

> The story of how local non-governmental organizations are creating wholistic, Caribbean-centered development alternatives to the policies of the countries of the North, the World Bank, and the IMF.

Sontheimer, Sally, ed. *Women and the Environment: A Reader: Crisis and Develzopment in the Third World.* New York: Monthly Review Press, 1992. $13.00.

> An informative and readable overview; authors represent many parts of the world.

South Commission. *The Challenge to the South.* Oxford: Oxford University Press, 1990.

> The South Commission was created in 1987 to present a perspective from the developing countries. Its most recent report is the best statement available of the concerns, hopes and plans of the Third World.

Poverty

Alternative Women-In-Development. *Reaganomics and Women: Structural Adjustment U.S. Style 1980-1992: A Case Study of Women and Poverty in the U.S.* Washington DC: Center of Concern, 1992. $4.50.

> This short document shows how "supply-side" economics have impoverished women in the U.S. in exactly the same way that policies in highly indebted nations have caused hardships for women in the "Two Thirds" world. Illustrated with charts and cartoons.

Aristide, Jean-Bertrand. Translated and edited by Amy Wilentz. *In The Parish of the Poor: Writings From Haiti.* Maryknoll: Orbis Books, 1991. $10.95.

> This book is a letter, written in solidarity with the disenfranchised in Latin America by the Roman Catholic priest who became the first freely elected president of Haiti. With compassion and sensitivity to the plight of the poor and powerless in a country with a history of corruption and violence, Father Aristide challenges injustices within his church and throughout Haiti.

Huntly, Alyson. *Rich World, Poor World: A Curriculum Resource on Youth and Development.* Dubuque, IA: Wm. C. Brown Company Publishers, 1987.

> Developed under the auspices of the Christian Movement for Peace in Canada, primarily for use in schools, this book is packed with information, biblical and faith reflections, and suggestions for action.

Mizuno, Michelle, ed. *Women, Poverty and the Economy.* Geneva: World Council of Churches, 1988. $6.50.

> This workbook compiles the testimonies of women and reports on women in poverty around the world from the World Council of Churches' Sub Unit on Women in Church and Society. Presented with pictures, poems, skits and prayers, the material offers a Christian reflection and response to this poverty, as well as an analysis of the socioeconomic issues as they affect women.

Women in Poverty: In Europe. Geneva: World Council of Churches, 1992. $5.50.

This is a collection of black and white photographs of and comments by European women. These women live in poverty and they tell their stories about debt, unemployment, exploitation, apathy, courage and generosity. The book offers a way to begin a discussion on women and the economy.

Material Wealth

Barlett, Donald L. and James B. Steele. *America: What Went Wrong?* Kansas City: Andrews and McMeel, 1992. $6.95.

Based on a popular series of *Philadelphia Inquirer* newspaper articles, this book examines recent economic trends which allowed Washington and Wall Street to dismantle the American middle class. The book describes how the U.S. lost a social contract in which all Americans can participate in economic growth. The book's many graphs supplement the easy-to-read text.

Galbraith, John Kenneth. *The Culture of Contentment.* New York: Houghton Mifflin Company, 1992. $22.95.

Galbraith shows how in the 1980s, the rich were bailed out, as in the savings and loan scandal, and the unemployed received nothing. Galbraith reveals how congressional inactivity, exploitative foreign policy and unnecessary weapons keep the fortunate people comfortable while the less fortunate majority are left out. (See also by Galbraith, *The Affluent Society,* 1963, an important book of its time.)

Lapham, Lewis. *Money and Class in America: Notes and Observations on the Civil Religion.* New York: Ballantine Books, 1988. $4.95.

This book is an essay on American's passion for money. Lapham tells stories concerning Americans' ambivalence regarding whether money is a virtue or a sin. He ends with an important question—"If we let go of our faith in money, who knows what we might put in its place?"

Neuhaus, Richard John. *Doing Well and Doing Good: The Challenge to the Christian Capitalist.* New York: Doubleday, 1992. $22.00.

An unapologetic neo-conservative vigorously supports democratic capitalism.

Economics from a Moral Perspective

Benne, Robert. *The Ethic of Democratic Capitalism: A Moral Reassessment.* Ann Arbor, MI: Books on Demand. $70.30.

A noteworthy defense of the market system.

De Santa Ana, Julio, ed. *Good News to the Poor: The Challenge of the Poor in the History of the Church.* Geneva: World Council of Churches, 1982. $7.95.

How does the church bring the Gospel's good news to the poor? This book adopts an historical perspective, exploring the challenges of the poor from the first four centuries to the late middle ages. The issues of hunger, liberation and development are very timely and familiar to us today. (A sequel to this book is *Separation Without Hope? The Church and the Poor During the Industrial Revolution and Colonial Expansion.* World Council of Churches, 1978. $7.95. Addresses church attitudes towards the poor and the oppressed from 1800 to 1914.)

Duchrow, Ulrich. *Global Economy: A Confessional Issues for the Churches?* Geneva: WCC Publications, 1987.

Chiefly addressing the affluent churches of the West, the author suggests how Christians from rich countries may become an ecumenical covenant people of God. He examines the politico-economic context of Western Europe through Scripture and the writings of Martin Luther, and finds that the ecumenical focus on justice, peace and the integrity of creation is the only saving course.

Ecumenical Coalition for Economic Justice. *Recolonization or Liberation: The Bonds of Structural Adjustment and Struggles for Emancipation.* Toronto, 1990.

Booklet examines structural adjustment programs from the perspective of those who are made to bear the burden of "adjustment" in many nations, including some in the industrialized world. It contends that there are viable alternatives to IMF and World Bank policies.

Greene, Bonnie, ed. *Canadian Churches and Foreign Policy*. Toronto: James Lorimer & Co., 1990.

Describes the need to learn to live with "enemies" and overcome the division of nations; examines some social and economic development issues, and summarizes the churches' work in human rights and corporate social responsibility. Contributors are notable church workers; appendices include 1989 discussion paper for the Canadian churches on the international debt crisis.

Haan, Roelf. *The Economics of Honour: Biblical Reflections on Money and Property*. Geneva: World Council of Churches, 1991. $6.50.

Fourteen meditations on biblical passages provide insight into economic life and injustice. Biblical passages provide spiritual critique of economic realities such as security and technology, commerce and development, production and distribution, wealth and poverty. Good for discussions in small study groups.

Klay, Robin Kendrick. *Counting the Cost: The Economics of Christian Stewardship*. Ann Arbor, MI: Books on Demand. $50.70.

A woman economist, writing from a Christian perspective, gives a nuanced defense of market capitalism.

Morgan, Elizabeth, with Van Weigel and Eric DeBaufre. *Global Poverty and Personal Responsibility: Integrity Through Commitment*. Mahway: Paulist Press, 1989. $9.95.

We can make a difference—that's the message of this book. It asks us to look at our actions, carry our concern to the world and then return to our communities and act responsibly. Each chapter ends with bibliography and questions for discussion. The book explains how the global is personal and the personal is global. Some practical suggestions include how to live simply and how to create communities.

Mulholland, Catherine, ed. *Ecumenical Reflections on Political Economy*. Geneva: WCC Publications, 1988.

Summarizes 10 years of work by the Advisory Group on Economic Matters (AGEM) of the Commission on the Churches' Participation in Development (CCPD) of the World Council of Churches. Highly readable, succinct analysis of global economic issues along with guidelines for the direction of change. Written by lay people, for Christians.

Nelson-Pallmeyer, Jack. *Brave New World Order*. Maryknoll: Orbis Books, 1992. $9.95.

Another perspective on how increased debt leads to increased death in the Third World.

Owensby, Walter L. *Economics for Prophets*. Grand Rapids, MI: William B. Eerdmans Publishing Co., 1988.

An excellent introduction to the study of market economics, including its global aspects, from one Christian perspective.

Schumacher, E.F. *Small Is Beautiful: Economics As If People Mattered*. New York: Harper and Row, 1973. $10.00.

A classic. Its refreshing approach to the world of economics is spiritual, human and environmental. For example, when asked for political advice based on his economic insights, Schumacher agreed with Gandhi, "Plant a tree."

Sen, Gita and Caren Grown. *Development, Crisis and Alternative Vision: Third World Women's Perspective*. New York: Monthly Review Press, 1987. $8.50.

Insights from Third World women who analyze development and crisis. Their alternative vision is actually a workable agenda.

Shaull, Richard. *Naming the Idols: Biblical Alternatives for U.S. Foreign Policy*. Oak Park, IL: Meyer-Stone Books, 1988. $9.95.

Exploring the biblical basis for helping the poor, Schaull contends that communion with the oppressed must be a primary spiritual concern. The book uses scriptural teachings to challenge U.S. foreign policy, especially in Central America. As a Presbyterian missionary in Latin America, Shaull writes compassionately of the poverty he witnesses when one country oppresses its neighbors.

Task Force on the Economic Crisis. *Intricate Web: Drugs and the Economic Crisis*. New York: General Board of Global Ministries of The United Methodist Church, 1990. $3.50.

A brief and readable introduction to the interconnections between drug abuse and the economic crisis around the world. Challenges Christians to wake up to the reality of drugs all around us, and to begin confronting the problem.

Zweig, Michael, ed. *Religion and Economic Justice*. Philadelphia, PA: Temple University Press, 1992.

Contributors from the fields of economics, religious ethics and biblical studies, critique the individualism which underlies mainstream economic analysis and which fragments our communities, and show that capitalism is no guarantee of prosperity.

FILMOGRAPHY

Primary Resources

A MATTER OF INTEREST
1/2" VHS   Sale: $19.95   1990   13:11

A delightful video that explains why, despite a dramatic increase in the world's money supply, the international debt just keeps on piling up. Many developing nations are technically bankrupt, while even in the so-called "developed" world we are starting to spend our grandchildren's inheritance. Some critical factors keep getting left out of the economic equations. Using simple animation, the video draws a parallel between life in debt-stricken countries and the plight of Maisy Mills, a woman who takes out a small-business mortgage and is hit by rising interest rates. The video raises ethical questions about lenders in rich countries demanding full repayment from poor countries, and encourages discussion about solutions to the debt crisis. Study guide included.
Available for sale only from:
Friendship Press Distribution Office
P.O. Box 37844
Cincinnati, OH 45222-0844
513-948-8733

Secondary Resources

BAREFOOT ECONOMIST
1/2" VHS   Rental: $50.00   1990   52:00

Manfred Max-Neef is a Chilean economist trying to address the problems of Latin America. Focus is on Chile, where Max-Neef uses approaches funded by international agencies to address the poverty and social upheaval created by rapid and uncontrolled development under a dictatorship. Max-Neef's vision is one of social justice.
Available from:
Landmark Films (see p. 119)

BRINGING IT ALL BACK HOME
1/2" VHS   Rental: $75   1987   48:00

This documentary analyzes how patterns of international capital investment and exploitation of Third World women workers in free trade zones are being brought home to the First World. Britain's declining industrial regions have been designated "enterprise zones" to attract multinational corporations. Not surprisingly, women again constitute the preferred labor force. Issues discussed include the internationalization of our local economies, the growing schism between the rich and poor, and the changing nature of women's work.
Available from:
Women Make Movies (see p. 119)

THE BUSINESS OF HUNGER
1/2" VHS   Rental: $15   1984   28:00

In many Third World countries, cash crops are exported while the poor go hungry. This phenomenon, one of the major causes of world hunger, is examined in Latin America, Africa, Asia, and the USA. The video proposes a more just distribution of the earth's resources, and offers a vision of a world where all have enough to eat.
Available from:
EcuFilm (see p. 119)

DEADLY DECEPTION: GENERAL ELECTRIC, NUCLEAR WEAPONS, AND OUR ENVIRONMENT
1/2" VHS   Sale: $25   1991   29:00
                Rental: $15

GE spends tens of million of dollars each year to polish its "We bring good things to life" image. Yet, the reality is that GE is the industry leader in producing critical components for nuclear weapons. GE has knowingly poisoned the environment and the people who work in or live near its facilities with deadly radiation and toxic waste. Video shows how to use resources wisely.
Available from:
INFACT (see p. 119)

THE DEBT CRISIS: AN AFRICAN DILEMMA
1/2" VHS   Sale: $125.00   20:00
                Rental: free loan

A look at an urbanized country, Zambia, which
shows how the debt crisis is a human issue in devel-
oping countries.
Available from:
   Mennonite Central Committee for rental (see
   p. 119)
   [**NOTE:** available from MCC office in
   Canada, as well]
Available from:
   Icarus/First Run for sale

THE DEBT CRISIS: AN UNNATURAL DISASTER
1/2" VHS   Sale: $39.95   1990   28:00
                Rental: $15.00

Using an engaging dramatic style, people from several Caribbean countries show how economic issues,
especially the worldwide debt crisis, affect their daily
lives. Attitudes from countries like the U.S. and Canada
are cleverly portrayed as well. An authentic look at
how people come to an understanding around complex issues. NOTE: This is a primary resource for the
Caribbean mission study theme. Study guide included.
Available from:
   FPDO for sale (see p. 117)
   EcuFilm for rental (see p. 119)

THE FLYING FARMER
1/2" VHS   Sale: $125.00
                Rental: $50.00   1989   27:00

Yage Prztyk, a Polish emigrant living in Quebec,
spends a portion of each year helping Peruvian coffee
growers in the Amazon jungles increase farm productivity, avoid pesticides, and secure the best market
prices. This video documents how one man can contribute to easing the world's problems, while exploring topics related to agriculture, health, economic development, international relations, and the environment.
Available from:
   First Run/Icarus Films (see p. 119)

GOD'S GLOBAL ECONOMY
1/2" VHS   Sale: $10.00   1991   14:30
                Rental: $3.00

A men's study group at a Presbyterian Church in
suburban Bedford, NY, looks at economic issues and
discovers some surprising conclusions about how global economic issues affect their own lives. Subject ties
in directly with the issues of this study theme; video
was produced primarily for men's groups. A study
guide booklet is available for an additional $3.00.
Available from:
   Presbyterian Publishing House (see p. 119)

LEARNING ECONOMICS: EMPOWERING
WOMEN FOR ACTION
1/2" VHS   Sale: $25.00   1991   25:00

This video depicts women sharing their stories
about developing economic literacy and putting the
science of economics into perspective. Issues addressed:
homelessness, lack of jobs, economic structures, affordable housing. Closely tied in to the issues of this study
theme. Facilitator's Guide study packet may accompany video at an additional cost.
Available from:
   Religious Network for Equality for Women
   (see p. 119)

TROUBLED HARVEST
1/2" VHS   Rental: $65.00   1990   30:00

Examines the lives of women migrant workers from
Mexico and Central America as they harvest fruit in
California and the Pacific Northwest. Reveals the dangerous effects of pesticides on their health and that of
their children, the problems they encounter as working mothers, and the destructive consequences of US
immigration policies on the unity of their families.
Available from:
   Women Make Movies (see p. 119)

Distributors

EcuFilm
810 Twelfth Avenue, South
Nashville, TN 37203
800-251-4091

First Run/Icarus Films
153 Waverly Place
New York, NY 10014
800-876-1710
212-727-1711

Friendship Press Distribution Office
P.O. Box 37844
Cincinnati, OH 45222-0844
513-948-8733

INFACT
256 Hanover Street
Boston, MA 02113
800-688-8797
617-742-4583

Landmark Films, Inc.
3450 Slade Run Drive
Falls Church, VA 22042
800-342-4336
703-536-9540

Mennonite Central Committee
Resource Library
21 South 12th Street
P.O. Box 500
Akron, PA 17501-0500
717-859-1151

MCC Saskatchewan
600-45th Street, West
Saskatoon, Saskatchewan S7L 5W9
CANADA
306-665-2555

Presbyterian Publishing House
100 Witherspoon Street
Louisville, KY 40202-1396
800-554-4694
    NOTE: item # for video: 18092002
           item # for booklet: 18092001

Religious Network for Equality for Women
Room 812A
475 Riverside Drive
New York, NY 10115
212-870-2995

Women Make Movies
Suite 206-7
225 Lafayette Street
New York, NY 10012
212-925-0606

ACKNOWLEDGMENTS

5   The RALL cartoon by Ted Rall is reprinted by permission of Chronicle Features.

7   Cartoon reprinted by permission of Carol-Simpson Productions

9-10   From "Ethiopian Oasis" by Robert M. Press. Reprinted by permission from *The Christian Science Monitor*. © 1991 The Christian Science Publishing Society. All rights reserved.

14   Cartoon reprinted by permission of Cartoonews, Inc.

17   KUDZU by Doug Marlette. By permission of Doug Marlette and Creators Sundicate.

19   The Bizarro cartoon by Dan Piraro is reprinted by permission of Chronicle Features, San Francisco, CA.

21   Cartoon reprinted by permission of Tribune Media Services.

23   Cartoon by Palomo reprinted by permission of Cartoonists & Writers Syndicate.

25   Cartoon by Shuto reprinted by permission of Cartoonists & Writers Syndicate.

27   Cartoon reprinted by permission of Tribune Media Services.

32   Cartoon reprinted by permission of Dogco Productions.

33   Cartoon by Gable. 1992 Cartoonists & Writers Sundicate.

40   Cartoon reprinted by permission of Mike Luckovich and Creators Syndicate.

41   Cartoon reprinted by permission of Dogco Productions.

44   PLANTU cartoon, Paris, France. Cartoonists & Writers Syndicate.

45   Cartoon reprinted with special permission of King Features Syndicate.

50   Cartoon reprinted by permission of Carol-Simpson Productions.

52   Cartoon reprinted by permission of Mike Luckovich and Creators Syndicate.

54   Cartoon reprinted by permission of the artist.

57   Cartoon by Danziger in *The Christian Science Monitor* © 1991 TCSPS.

58   KAL cartoon reprinted by permission of Cartoonists & Writers Syndicate.

61   Cartoon reprinted by permission of *The Buffalo News*

62   Cartoon by Gomas reprinted by permission of Cartoonists & Writers Syndicate.

64   Cartoon reprinted by permission of Carol-Simpson Productions.

65   Cartoon reprinted by permission of Cartoonews, Inc.

69   Cartoon copyright 1984, Boston Globe. Distributed by Los Angeles Times Syndicate. Reprinted with permission.

71-72   Quotation from *Economics for Prophets* by Walter Owensby. Reprinted by permission of Wm. B. Eerdmans Publishing Co.

72   Cartoon from *The Wall Street Journal*—Permission, Cartoon Features Syndicate.

73   Cartoon copyright 1990, Boston Globe. Distributed by Los Angeles Times Syndicate. Reprinted with permission.

79   Cartoon reprinted by permission of Carol-Simpson Productions.

83   Cartoon reprinted by permission of *The Buffalo News*.

85   Cartoon by Bado reprinted by permission of Cartoonists & Writers Syndicate.

88   Cartoon reprinted by permission of Carol-Simpson Productions.

93   Cartoon reprinted by permission of Carol-Simpson Productions.

101   Cartoon reprinted by permission of *The Buffalo News*.